A GREATER

democracy

DAY BY DAY

A GREATER
democracy
DAY BY DAY

Sally Mahé and Kathy Covert

Council Oak Books

San Francisco / Tulsa

Publishers have generously given permission to use extended quotations from the following copyrighted works. From *The American Soul* by Jacob Needleman, © 2002 by Jacob Needleman. Used by permission of Jeremy P. Tarcher, an imprint of Penguin Group (USA) Inc. From *Granny D* by Doris Haddock and Dennis Burke, © 2001 by Doris Haddock and Dennis Burke. Used by permission of Villard Books, a division of Random House, Inc. From *Jazz: A History of America's Music* by Geoffrey C. Ward and Ken Burns, © 2000 by The Jazz Film Project, Inc. Used by permission of Alfred A. Knopf, a division of Random House, Inc. From *Free Play: Improvisations in Life and Art* by Stephen Nachmanovitch, © 1990 by Stephen Nachmanovitch. Used by permission of Penguin Group (USA) Inc. From *I Dream a World: Portraits of Black Women Who Changed America* by Brian Lanker, edited by Barbara Summers, © 1989. Used by permission of Stewart, Tabori & Chang.

ISBN 1-57178-166-8

To our mothers.
To the children who will inherit our Earth.

contents

preface

This unique collection of ideas about democracy is meant to lift our spirits and remind us that there is power in our hearts to create the world we want for coming generations. Our intention in gathering these ideas is to offer a simple gift to good-hearted people in the United States and all over the world. These ideas are given to remind us of what is possible and convince us that we, the people, all of us, make a difference that counts. I hope the diverse voices in this book inspire each of us to take actions that bring beauty, dignity, justice, and healing to the world. We can do it. Now is the time.

With gratitude to all visionaries of democracy,
Sally Mahé

This book is Sally's idea. She invited me to join her on this project – in part because in a brief biographical sketch I described myself as a "citizen." And, as a citizen, wife, daughter, sister, and friend how could I say anything but "yes!" when invited to reintroduce the provocative proposition of democracy to my fellow Americans?

Our deepest desire is for readers everywhere to rediscover the power of the provocative proposition that we are all created equal and all deserve to share in the bounty of this Earth.

With gratitude,
Kathy Covert

introduction

This book is neither a single treatise on democracy nor a history of its development. Instead, it is a collection of provocative and inspiring quotations, poems, stories, and songs. Like "fingers pointing to the moon" these selections point to the essence of a greater democracy – one that works for everyone. We invite you to regard this collection as you would a trusted friend who guides and nudges you when life becomes difficult and filled with doubt.

We all know that we live in a world blessed with abundant natural resources, beauty, and vibrant, diverse peoples. And yet, we also experience accelerating inequality, the effects of war and environmental degradation, and a universal longing to be "free from want and fear."

Because democracy is a human institution, it can fall short of our highest expectations, be too narrowly construed, be experienced as cumbersome, and otherwise show its vulnerability to human failings. And yet the promise of greater democracy continues to prompt ordinary people to bring the "angels of their better nature" to the challenges they face.

As pragmatic visionaries, democracy's advocates know that creating a greater democracy takes effort and time. But we deeply believe that we experience the best of what it means to be human through active, creative engagement not only with family, friends, and fellow citizens but with our adversaries, too.

Also, we profoundly trust that democracy continues to evolve and provide our greatest hope for governing our communities, our regions, and our nations wisely – and that it is within our power to defend and call forth these blessings in our great nation and around the world.

Because we are as always poised on a threshold of possibilities, and there appears to be an unquenchable readiness, no matter how challenging, to begin anew, we offer this multi-faceted collection for your reflection. In addition, since democracy has so many sources and dimensions, the book is arranged by enduring democratic themes – one for each month – which allow us to view democracy's rich character in a fresh light.

Thus we invite you to connect these ideas with your own and to share them with others. After all, in the words of Doris Haddock (better known as Granny D), democracy is "exquisitely personal to each of us."

JANUARY

roots and wings

Hundreds of years ago native peoples of the northeastern woodlands of
North America lived with respect for the land and practiced basic
principles of democracy. Centuries earlier, in ancient Greece, philosophers, statesmen, and citizens practiced fundamental values of democracy through
forms such as jury courts and rigorous civic discourse, leaving us with a great
legacy of democratic principles.

In the late 18th century, leaders of American independence integrated some of
these ideas into their own high ideals of equality, human rights, liberty, and self-
governance. These principles, which became the founding values embodied in the
Constitution of the United States, still live in our land and in our hearts. They
have been both illuminated and contested by leaders and ordinary people in every
generation and are put into action by citizens every day. These perspectives — not
least when they are under assault — strengthen us with visions of a greater democracy and spur our participation. As we wonder how to advance and preserve
democratic principles amid today's reality and for tomorrow's world, these offer-
ings can serve as our roots and wings.

January 1

The early history, long before the Indo-Europeans came, explains that there was a time when the people of the North American forest experienced war and strife. It was at that time that there came into this land one who carried words and plans of peace – one who would come to be called the Peacemaker. . . . He traveled among the people, going from nation to nation, seeking those who would take up his way of peace. Eventually five nations, the Mohawks, Oneidas, Onondagas, Cayugas, and Senecas, were the initial ones to take up the offer of peace. These nations gathered together in council and there they set down the principles of what is called the Gayaneshakgowa, or the Great Law of Peace [known also as The Constitution of the Iroquois Confederacy].

A Basic Call to Consciousness,
The Haudenosaunee Address to the Western World

January 2

It shall be the duty of all of the chiefs of the League of Five Nations from time to time as occasion demands to act as teachers and spiritual guides of their people and remind them of their Creator's will and words. They shall say:

Listen, that peace may continue into future days!

Always listen to the words of the Great Creator, for he has spoken. United people, let no evil find lodging in your minds.

The Great Creator has spoken and the cause of peace shall not become old.

The cause of peace shall not die if you remember the Great Creator.

CONSTITUTION OF THE IROQUOIS CONFEDERACY

JANUARY 3

[To the chiefs it was said] . . . you shall become a mentor of the people of the Five Nations . . . you shall be filled with peace and goodwill and your mind filled with a yearning for the welfare of the people of the confederacy.

With endless patience you shall carry out your duty and your firmness shall be tempered with tenderness for your people. Neither anger nor fury shall lodge in your mind and all your words and actions shall be marked with calm deliberation. In all your deliberation in the Council, in your efforts at lawmaking, in all of your official acts, self-interest shall be cast in oblivion. Cast not away the warnings of others, if they should chide you for any error or wrong you may do, but return to the way of the Great Law, which is just and right.

CONSTITUTION OF THE IROQUOIS CONFEDERACY

JANUARY 4

. . . Look and listen for the welfare of the whole people and have always in view not only the present but also the coming generations even those whose faces are yet beneath the surface of the earth – the unborn of the future nation.

CONSTITUTION OF THE IROQUOIS CONFEDERACY

JANUARY 5

*T*he history of every country begins in the heart of a man or a woman.

WILLA CATHER, AUTHOR

JANUARY 6

*D*emocracy is the self-creating process of life appearing as the true nature of man, and through the activity of man projecting itself into the visible world in fitting form so that its essential oneness will declare itself. Democracy then is not an end. We must be weaving all the time the web of democracy.

MARY PARKER FOLLETT, VISIONARY

JANUARY 7

I have deep faith that the principle of the universe will be beautiful and simple.

ALBERT EINSTEIN, PHYSICIST

JANUARY 8

*E*very history of the creation and every traditional account, whether from the lettered or the unlettered world . . . all agree on establishing one point . . . that all men are of *one degree* and consequently that all men are born equal, and with equal natural rights; in the same manner . . . every child born into the world must be considered as deriving its existence from God. The world is as new to him as it was to the first man that existed, and his natural right in it is of the same kind.

THOMAS PAINE, STATESMAN

JANUARY 9

A popular government without popular information, or the means of acquiring it, is but a prologue to a farce or a tragedy; or perhaps, both. Knowledge will forever govern ignorance. And a people who mean to be their own governors must arm themselves with the power that knowledge gives.

JAMES MADISON, US PRESIDENT, 1809-1817

JANUARY 10

*W*e hold these truths to be self-evident, that all men are created equal, that they are endowed by their Creator with certain unalienable rights, that among these are life, liberty, and the pursuit of happiness. That to secure these rights, governments are instituted among men, deriving their just powers from the consent of the governed. That whenever any form of government becomes destructive of these ends, it is the right of the people to alter and to abolish it, and to institute new government, laying its foundation on such principles and organizing its powers in such form as to them shall seem most likely to effect their safety and happiness.

DECLARATION OF INDEPENDENCE UNITED STATES OF AMERICA

JANUARY 11

*T*he independence of America, considered merely as a separation from England, would have been a matter of but little importance, had it not been accompanied by a revolution in the principles and practices of governments. She made a stand, not for herself only, but for the world, and looked beyond the advantages she herself could receive.

THOMAS PAINE, STATESMAN

JANUARY 12

*W*e will never know what we have here if we do not understand that the founding basis of this country was not land or tribe, but the call for people to assemble together and work together for the good.

JACOB NEEDLEMAN, PHILOSOPHER

JANUARY 13

*A*merican democracy is a transcendent notion positing that power flows not from without but from within. It was not to be the wealth or power of one's outer circumstances, but the spirit of intelligent goodness which resides inside us all that was entrusted with the authority to rule this nation.

MARIANNE WILLIAMSON, AUTHOR

JANUARY 14

*I*n the Constitution, the founding fathers gave to the world the architecture of freedom, dignity and happiness – a structure that, like no other before it, allows the possibility of human fulfillment. Yet the structure does not have the power in and of itself to guarantee the freedom and happiness it stands for. The flame in the hearth has to come from elsewhere, from deeper than the most brilliant rational thought – from our relationship to something unspeakable, which transcends us.

ROGER HOUSDEN, AUTHOR

January 15

*N*ow is the time to make real the promise of democracy and transform our pending national elegy into a creative psalm of brotherhood.

MARTIN LUTHER KING, JR., CIVIL RIGHTS LEADER

January 16

*W*e, the people of the United States, in order to form a more perfect union, establish justice, insure domestic tranquility, provide for the common defense, promote the general welfare, and secure the blessings of liberty to ourselves and our posterity, do ordain and establish this Constitution for the United States of America.

PREAMBLE, UNITED STATES CONSTITUTION

JANUARY 17

*I*n one way or another, this is the oldest story in America: the struggle to determine whether "we, the people" is a spiritual idea embedded in a political reality – one nation, indivisible – or merely a charade masquerading as piety and manipulated by the powerful and privileged to sustain their own way of life at the expense of others.

BILL MOYERS, JOURNALIST

JANUARY 18

*A*s for the idea of democracy, the founding fathers – Washington, Jefferson, Franklin and others – never conceived of it solely as an external form of government. The meaning of democracy was always rooted in a vision of human nature as both fallible and perfectible. To a significant extent, democracy in its specifically American form was created to allow men and women to seek their own higher principles within themselves. Without that inner meaning, democracy becomes, as Plato and Aristotle pointed out 2,500 years ago, a celebration of disorder and superficiality.

JACOB NEEDLEMAN, PHILOSOPHER

JANUARY 19

*D*emocracy . . . a charming form of government, full of variety and disorder, and dispensing a sort of equality to equals and unequals alike.

PLATO, PHILOSOPHER

JANUARY 20

*H*ere [in Athens] each individual is interested not only in his own affairs but in the affairs of the city as well . . . we do not say that a man who takes no interest in politics minds his own business, we say he has no business here at all . . .

PERICLES, STATESMAN

January 21

*T*he Athenians finally lost out to other great empires [in part] because they failed to find ways to allow the true power of the citizen community to continuously evolve. . . . Athenian society included women, slaves, resident foreigners and even imperial subjects. Many individuals among these non-citizen groups had proved remarkably loyal to Athens in times of crisis . . . yet with only limited exceptions Athenian citizenship remained the jealously guarded privilege of native born men.

BROOK MANVILLE AND JOSIAH OBER, AUTHORS

January 22

*D*emocracy and the one, the ultimate ideal of humanity, are synonyms. The idea of democracy, the ideas of liberty, equality, and fraternity, represent a society in which the distinction between the spiritual and the secular has ceased.

JOHN DEWEY, EDUCATOR AND PHILOSOPHER

January 23

The care of human life and happiness, and not their destruction, is the first and only object of good government.

THOMAS JEFFERSON, US PRESIDENT, 1801-1809

January 24

There will never be a better world until there are better people in it. In order for that to occur, we must all start with ourselves. And, in doing so, we become, in a sense, co-creators with God – co-creators of a renewed world on its way to paradise, as it was in the beginning. And, therefore, as it was in our mythic beginning, we should all say to ourselves. "Let there be light and let it begin with me."

JOHN WHITE, AUTHOR

JANUARY 25

The Light That Fills the World

I think over again
My small adventures, my fears.
The small ones that seemed so big,
For all the vital things I had to get and to reach.
And yet there is only one great thing, the only thing:
To live to see the great day that dawns,
And the light that fills the world.

OLD INUIT SONG

JANUARY 26

In the forests of the River Amazon, as on the crest of the High Andes, I realized how, from pole to pole, as though animated by a single breath, one life alone is diffused among stones, plants, animals and the swelling breast of man.

TEILHARD DE CHARDIN, PALEONTOLOGIST

JANUARY 27

*T*hen I was standing on the highest mountain of them all, and round about beneath me was the whole hoop of the world. And while I stood there I saw more than I can tell and I understood more than I saw; for I was seeing in a sacred manner the shapes of all things in the spirit, and the shapes of all shapes as they live together like one being. And I saw the sacred hoop of my people was one of many hoops that made one circle, wide as daylight and as starlight, and in the center grew one mighty flowering tree to shelter all the children of one mother and one father. And I saw that it was holy . . . But anywhere is the center of the world.

BLACK ELK, HOLY MAN, OGLALA SIOUX

JANUARY 28

*W*hen America does recognize its need for others we shall be completing the circle. You see this paradigm means that nations can meet each other in new relationship. The strong gives the best it has, and receives the best that the weak has. For me, this is democracy in its deepest sense.

ABDUL AZIZ SAID, PROFESSOR INTERNATIONAL RELATIONS

JANUARY 29

*I*f liberty and equality, as is thought by some, are chiefly to be found in democracy, they will be best attained when all persons alike share in the government to the utmost.

ARISTOTLE, PHILOSOPHER

JANUARY 30

A free society is one where it is safe to be unpopular.

ADLAI STEVENSON, STATESMAN

JANUARY 31

The simple truth – a gorgeous earth drifts light as a feather around the great roaring generosity of the sun. The sun's story will find its climax in a story from the human family – of those women and men whose lives manifested the same generosity and whose sacrifice enabled others to reach fulfillment. If, through the ages, the various cultures have admired such people who poured out their creative energies so that others might live – we were only intuitively recognizing that such humans were true to the energy that filled them.

BRIAN SWIMME, COSMOLOGIST

FEBRUARY

Courage

What does courage have to do with democracy? Everything.

Courage enables us as individuals, neighbors, and fellow citizens to step toward the unknown with confidence and resolve.

The root definition of courage is the French word coeur, meaning heart. Courage, which lives at the base of the human heart, is the armament that enables us to face both private and public fears, and to fight for a better life for ourselves and others in our communities and around the world. In a greater democracy, courage is "of the people," which means that we are expected to live courageously and help each other grow strong.

In the spirit of Native American elder Maria José Hobday, who counsels us to "lift up your heartbone," the following quotes encourage us to follow her advice and cast off the impediments of dismay, passivity, and fear.

FEBRUARY 1

It is from numberless diverse acts of courage and belief that human history is shaped.

ROBERT F. KENNEDY, US ATTORNEY GENERAL

FEBRUARY 2

I perceive mighty dangers which it is possible to ward off, mighty evils which may be avoided, and I cling with a firmer hold to the belief that for democratic nations to be virtuous and prosperous – they require but the will to do it.

ALEXIS DE TOCQUEVILLE, HISTORIAN

FEBRUARY 3

What after all had maintained the human race on this globe, despite all the calamities of nature and all the tragic failings of mankind, if not the faith in new possibilities and the courage to advocate them?

JANE ADDAMS, SOCIAL WORKER

FEBRUARY 4

*O*ut of all the pain caused by hatred and injustice in our nation's history, there has emerged another more hopeful narrative. It is a narrative composed by men and women who refused to allow their humanity to be diminished by others.

MARIA FLEMING, COMMUNITY ORGANIZER

FEBRUARY 5

*T*o live the full life one must have the courage to bear the responsibility of the needs of others . . .

AUNG SUNG SUU KYI, PRO-DEMOCRACY ACTIVIST

FEBRUARY 6

*I*t depends upon what each of us does, what we consider democracy means and what we consider freedom in a democracy means and whether we really care about it enough to face ourselves and our prejudices and to make up our minds what we really want our nation to be, and what its relationship is to be to the rest of the world. The day we know that we'll be moral and spiritual leaders.

ELEANOR ROOSEVELT, A CO-AUTHOR OF
UNIVERSAL DECLARATION OF HUMAN RIGHTS

FEBRUARY 7

*A*merica is a nation founded on a vision of faith and hope in the capacity of people for self-governance. Fear was not the model upon which America was founded. Even amid the crucible of real international threats and conflicts, the founders of America were governed by profound insights into the human condition and the importance of having a sense of humility.

JONATHAN GRANOFF, PRESIDENT GLOBAL SECURITY INSTITUTE

FEBRUARY 8

You cannot fight by being on the outside complaining and whining. You have to get on the inside to be able to assess their strengths and weaknesses and then move in.

SHIRLEY CHISHOLM, US CONGRESSWOMAN

FEBRUARY 9

I think that black women, whether they were strong or whether they were beaten and broken down, had a belief in goodness of the future. They always wanted another world that would be better for their children than it had been for them. The black woman has deep wells of spiritual strength. She doesn't know how she is going to feed her family in the morning, but she prays and in the morning, out of thin air, she makes breakfast.

MARGARET WALKER ALEXANDER, POET

FEBRUARY 10

I'd tell the children of the future that they have to stand up for their rights. They have an idea they can. But I feel that they are shadows underneath a great shelter and that they need to come forth and stand up for some of the things that are right.

SEPTIMA POINSETTE CLARK, CIVIL RIGHTS TEACHER

FEBRUARY 11

I wanted you to see what real courage is instead of getting the idea that courage is a man with a gun in his hand. It's when you know you're licked before you begin but you begin anyway and you see it through no matter what.

HARPER LEE, AUTHOR

FEBRUARY 12

*A*lways bear in mind that your own resolution to succeed is more important than any other one thing.

ABRAHAM LINCOLN, US PRESIDENT, 1861-1865

FEBRUARY 13

*N*ever be discouraged from being an activist because people tell you that you'll not succeed. You have already succeeded if you're out there representing truth or justice or compassion or fairness or love. You already have your victory because you have changed the world; you have changed the status quo by you; you have changed the chemistry of things. And changes will spread from you, will be easier to happen again in others because of you, because, believe it or not, you are the center of the world.

DORIS HADDOCK, POLITICAL ACTIVIST

FEBRUARY 14

*T*here is plenty of courage among us for the abstract, but not for the practical.

HELEN KELLER, HUMANITARIAN

FEBRUARY 15

*C*autious, careful people always casting about to preserve their reputations or social standards never can bring about reform.

SUSAN B, ANTHONY, SUFFRAGIST

FEBRUARY 16

*N*ow is no time to think of what you do not have. Think of what you can do with what there is.

ERNEST HEMINGWAY, AUTHOR

FEBRUARY 17

*W*e cannot escape fear. We can only transform it into a companion that accompanies us on all of our exciting adventures. Take a risk a day, one small or bold stroke that will make you feel great once you've done it.

SUSAN JEFFERS, AUTHOR

FEBRUARY 18

here is no perfect time to get involved in social causes, no ideal circumstances for voicing our convictions. Instead, each of us faces a lifelong series of imperfect moments in which we must decide what to stand for. We may have to seek them out consciously, sometimes in discouraging contexts or when we don't feel ready. The wonder is that when we do begin to act, we often gain the knowledge, confidence, and strength that we need to continue.

PAUL LOEB, SOCIAL PSYCHOLOGIST

FEBRUARY 19

ntil one is committed, there is hesitancy, the chance to draw back, always ineffectiveness. Concerning all acts of initiative (and creation), there is one elementary truth the ignorance of which kills countless ideas and splendid plans: that the moment one definitely commits oneself, then providence moves too. All sorts of things occur to help one that would never otherwise have occurred. A whole stream of events issues from the decision, raising in one's favor all manner of unforeseen incidents and meetings and material assurance, which no man could have dreamed would have come his way.

Whatever you can do or dream you can, begin it.
Boldness has genius, power and magic in it.
Begin it now.

JOHANN WOLFGANG VON GOETHE, POET AND DRAMATIST

FEBRUARY 20

*P*eople who love soft words and hate iniquity forget this – that reform consists in taking a bone away from a dog. Philosophy will not do this.

JOHN JAY CHAPMAN, POLITICAL REFORMER

FEBRUARY 21

*T*rickle down politics doesn't work much better than trickle down economics. It's also a fact that civilization happens because we don't leave things to other people. What's right and good doesn't come naturally. You have to stand up and fight for it as if the cause depends on you, because it does.

BILL MOYERS, JOURNALIST

FEBRUARY 22

I think that the hardest thing today is that, in both our personal and public lives, the status quo seems so permanent. It looks as though what we see around us is the way it has to be. I think the first step is for each of us to realize that this system is brand new on the planet. We created it only recently . . . and its sense of permanence and power is an illusion. If we appreciate this, we can liberate ourselves from false mythology. We can realize that history could conceivably have been very different. It still can. How did people do away with the divine right of kings? They simply stopped believing in it.

FRANCES MOORE LAPPÉ, FOUNDER CENTER FOR LIVING DEMOCRACY

FEBRUARY 23

Some believe there is nothing one man or one woman can do against the enormous array of the world's ills. Yet many of the world's great movements, of thought and action, have flowed from the work of a single man (or woman). A young monk began the Protestant reformation, a young general extended an empire from Macedonia to the borders of the earth, and a young woman reclaimed the territory of France. It was a young Italian explorer who discovered the New World, and the thirty-two-year-old Thomas Jefferson who proclaimed that all men are created equal.

ROBERT F. KENNEDY, US ATTORNEY GENERAL

FEBRUARY 24

The Elm Dance

Following my eyes, Vladimir Ilyich said, "That is where the children may not go – or any of us, for that matter. You see, the trees stay radioactive a long time. Our ancestors were of the forest. . . . Even in the hardest times under Stalin, we went into the woodlands every holiday, every weekend – walking, picnicking, mushrooming. Yes, we were always people of the forest." Quietly he repeated, "people of the forest."

I asked him, "When will you be able to go back into the forest?" With a tired little smile he shrugged. "Not in my lifetime," he said, and looking at his grandson, he added, "and not in his lifetime either." Then he gestured to the wallpaper. "This is our forest now."

It is the second morning of our three days together, and the people entering the school assembly room take each other's hands and, before any words are spoken, move into the Elm Dance. Every fourth measure, between moving right or left, forwards or backwards, we pause for four beats, gently swaying. To my eyes this morning, we could be trees, slender trunks swaying from firm roots, and our arms, as we raise them, look like branches meeting, interlacing. Do we dance for the forests we can no longer enter?

As I circle in step with all the others, I recall the connections that brought me this dance – how it came to me from Hannelore, my friend in Germany, who received it from Anastasia, her German friend, who created it from the Latvian song. The dance is not only for the healing of the elm, said Anastasia to Hannelore to me. It is for intention. It is to strengthen our capacity to choose a purpose, and to follow through on the resolve our hearts have made.

JOANNA MACY, BUDDHIST SCHOLAR AND ECO-PHILOSOPHER

FEBRUARY 25

*Y*ou are going to live in a dangerous world for quite a while I guess, but it's going to be an interesting and adventurous one. I wish you the courage to face it. I wish you the courage to face yourselves and when you know what you really want to fight for, not in a war but in order to gain a peace, then I wish you imagination and understanding. God bless you. May you win.

ELEANOR ROOSEVELT, A CO-AUTHOR OF
UNIVERSAL DECLARATION OF HUMAN RIGHTS

FEBRUARY 26

*W*here does the strength come from to see the race to the end? It comes from within.

CHARIOTS OF FIRE, BRITISH FILM

FEBRUARY 27

Hope
A simple four letter word so powerful
It can subdue despair
Confidence can rise
And courage goes forth and becomes the burning flame
To fan the heart onward.

HOWARD T. RAINER, POET

FEBRUARY 28

. . . the gains made by democracy, which are the gains made by human beings over themselves, are never static. We fight for them and have to keep on fighting. The gains are slow and are won in day by day effort.

ELEANOR ROOSEVELT, A CO-AUTHOR OF
UNIVERSAL DECLARATION OF HUMAN RIGHTS

FEBRUARY 29

It's coming like the tidal flood
Beneath the lunar sway,
Imperial, mysterious,
In amorous array:
Democracy is coming to the USA

LEONARD COHEN, POET

MARCH

Every Voice

Whose voice is heard? Whose voice counts? The story of democracy is one of an ever-expanding chorus of voices. In the beginning we hear only wealthy white male voices. And then, over time, the voices of white women could be heard. More time passed and the voices of black men and women joined the chorus. Rich and poor, white and black, men and women, urban and rural, left and right. The most beautiful music starts with a harmonious blend of opposites. Just imagine the song we will sing when the voices of the flowers, trees, butterflies, buffaloes and bees hum along with us. This is the time arrow of democracy made manifest, a rich diversity of voices speaking and being heard. Halleluiah!

MARCH 1

*L*ift every voice and sing till Earth and heaven ring, ring with harmonies of liberty . . .

"Black national anthem," official song of the NAACP

MARCH 2

*U*se every occasion to express your fundamental beliefs and dreams. Affirm to others the vision of the world you want. Network through action, network through love, network through spirit. You are the center of the network. You are a free and powerful source of life and goodness. Affirm it. Spread it. Radiate it. Time is now – we are the leaders we have been waiting for.

Robert Muller, Assistant Secretary-General, United Nations

MARCH 3

I have spent my days stringing and unstringing my instrument while the song I came to sing remains unsung.

Rabindranath Tagore, mystic

MARCH 4

*W*hen a song is in you, you've got to sing it.

CATO, 19TH-CENTURY AMERICAN FIELD SLAVE

MARCH 5

*E*very person matters. In that single thought lies the oral authority of American democracy.

MARIANNE WILLIAMSON, AUTHOR

MARCH 6

*L*et the voices of all of the people be heard.

NELSON MANDELA, PRESIDENT, SOUTH AFRICA, 1994-1999

*I*t is at once the weakness and the strength of democracy, its danger and its glory, that the fate of its members lies largely in their own hands. Where government rests ultimately upon the participation of the governed, it is their wisdom, collectively formed and expressed, that must determine its failure or success.

CARL COHEN, AUTHOR

MARCH 8

*W*e have sung ourselves awake. We have called ourselves to action.

ANONYMOUS

MARCH 9

*T*hese virtues – free inquiry, toleration of diverse opinion, and free communication – are necessary if not sufficient attributes of a democratic society and polity. . . . As "laboratories of knowledge," schools should engage children in on-going experimentation, communication, [and] self-criticism – so that the students constitute themselves as a youthful commonwealth of cooperative inquiry.

JOHN DEWEY, PHILOSOPHER AND EDUCATOR

MARCH 10

*N*othing appears more surprising to those who consider human affairs with a philosophical eye, than the easiness with which the many are governed by the few.

DAVID HUME, PHILOSOPHER

March 11

*F*reedom is when the people can speak; democracy is when the government listens.

ALASTAIR FARRUGIA, COMPUTER PROGRAMMER

March 12

*A*s I listen, the great chorus of life and joy begins again, and amid the awful orchestra of seen and unseen powers and destinies of good and evil our trumpets sound once more a note of daring, hope and will.

OLIVER WENDELL HOLMES, JR. SUPREME COURT JUSTICE

March 13

*W*ho is a wise person? One who learns from all people.

THE TALMUD

MARCH 14

What is the source of our first suffering? It lies in the fact that we hesitated to speak. It was born in the moment when we accumulated silent things within us.

GASTON BACHELARD, FRENCH THINKER

MARCH 15

The ultimate sign of human progress is a world where people, not just scientists and corporate chiefs, but all of the people, are allowed to make decisions that affect their lives.

JAY WALLJASPER, EDITOR

MARCH 16

All change in history, all advance, comes from the non-conformity. If there had been no troublemakers, no dissenters, we should still be living in caves.

ALAN JOHN PERCIVALE TAYLOR, HISTORIAN

MARCH 17

*T*he priceless heritage of our society is the unrestricted constitutional right of each member to think as he will. Thought control is a copyright of totalitarianism, and we have no claim to it. It is not the function of our government to keep the citizen from falling into error; it is the function of the citizen to keep the government from falling into error.

ROBERT H. JACKSON, SUPREME COURT JUSTICE

MARCH 18

I envision an America in 2020 that values each citizen equally and believes that harmony can exist within a robust diversity.

ANDREW LUXEN, YOUNG DEMOCRATIC VISIONARY

MARCH 19

*W*e believe that democratic wisdom can arise only from the informed dialogue, deliberation and reflection among diverse citizens. Our diversity and common ground are to be equally treasured as resources in our exercise of democratic imagination.

TOM ATLEE, FOUNDER, CO-INTELLIGENCE INSTITUTE

MARCH 20

*I*t's much easier to assume that the great peacemakers – and the ordinary ones in our families and neighborhoods – are different from the rest of us. It is easier to assume that something sets us apart from the likes of Aldo Leopold or Rachel Carson than it is to try to speak up for people and nature with our own voices.

BETH SAWIN, BIOLOGIST

MARCH 21

*W*hat we *are* clear about is the need to open what has been closed, reveal what has been hidden, substitute human choice for subhuman fate, and draw all manner of untouchables from the periphery into the center where the choices seem to be made.

HARLAN CLEVELAND, PUBLIC EXECUTIVE AND VISIONARY

MARCH 22

We are not draft eligible numbers, or ten digit call back numbers, or 26 digit credit card numbers or weekly unemployed numbers, we are not ledger numbers or ciphers, or percents of GDP, or construction starts, we are people!

CRAIG BARNES, POLITICAL COMMENTATOR

MARCH 23

Democracy is participation.

LINDA L. NELSON, RENOVATOR OF SMALL TOWN OPERA HOUSE

MARCH 24

We grow up in this culture learning basic skills like reading, writing, arithmetic, but there's very little emphasis on the skills we call the arts of democracy. How well do we listen? How well do we participate in envisioning a future? How well do we support people taking on new roles, like speaking in public for the first time? How well do we use conflict as a source of creativity rather than something to run from? And how well are we able to tolerate uncertainty, because living democracy is a process whose very nature is uncertain and dynamic?

FRANCES MOORE LAPPÉ, FOUNDER, CENTER FOR LIVING DEMOCRACY

MARCH 25

The work people do in these settings [grassroots natural resource coalitions] requires them to listen closely and actively to people they have never liked or trusted, to see if they can find some grain of insight which might open a pathway to a mutually beneficial solution.

DANIEL KEMMIS, DIRECTOR, CENTER FOR THE ROCKY MOUNTAIN WEST

MARCH 26

Participation in the political process does not require us to sink to dirty politics or reduce our vision to sound bites. As our circle of compassion has expanded, so have our capacities to keep ego from dominating the world, to build movements based on distributed power, to listen deeply to the fears and the hopes of those we are trying to reach, and to choose language that communicates our common humanity and aspirations.

SARAH RUTH VAN GELDER, EDITOR

MARCH 27

*O*ur lives begin to end the day we become silent about things that matter.

MARTIN LUTHER KING, JR., CIVIL RIGHTS LEADER

MARCH 28

I recently have perceived that the flame I most reductively and truly am is not going to flicker out. I am and that's that.

ANNE TRUITT, ARTIST

MARCH 29

*P*laying small doesn't serve the world. There's nothing enlightened about shrinking so that other people won't feel insecure around you. We were born to make manifest the glory of God that is within us. It's not just in some of us; it's in everyone. And, as we let our own light shine, we unconsciously give other people permission to do the same. As we are liberated from our own fear, our presence automatically liberates others.

MARIANNE WILLIAMSON, AUTHOR

MARCH 30

*P*eople count. The voice of wise and compassionate citizens may start to ring the bell of others. Citizenship, solidarity and an appreciative approach to others may generate the needed wave of spiritual revolution.

ANDRÉ PORTO, SPIRITUAL ACTIVIST

MARCH 31

*A*nd then compassion will be wedded to power . . . and then both men and women will be gentle. And both women and men will be strong . . . and no person will be subject to another's will.

JUDY CHICAGO, ARTIST

A P R I L

Out of Many, One

E Pluribus Unum. Out of many, one. What a powerful idea!

Out of many human beings, one family
Out of many families, one community
Out of many communities, one region
Out of many regions, one nation,
Out of many nations, one world.

We are all unique individuals and, at the same time, integral "parts" of ever larger wholes. How can we find common ground in the midst of such rich diversity? By choosing to act out of enlightened self-interest and with a healthy respect for civic life. By bringing a generosity of spirit to the nexus of private and public life we enliven the American experiment. Our collective actions help create a greater democracy.

A P R I L   1

The motto of the United States – E Pluribus Unum – means "out of many, one." This . . . process, an emergence . . . happens over and over, never reducing the many to one, nor the one to many. . . . Deep democracy comes to life through hearing diverse perspectives and exploring together, in shared reflection. . . . Out of many, one . . . is also the essence of peace in a world of differences.

TOM ATLEE, FOUNDER, CO-INTELLIGENCE INSTITUTE

A P R I L   2

Let us put our minds together and see what kind of life we can make for our children.

SITTING BULL, LAKOTA CHIEF

APRIL 3

This is the second American Revolution – that we will secure our future through the quality of our being, through the nature of our community, and through our relationships. Rather than pledging our credit we will pledge our trust in each other as human beings.

CRAIG BARNES, POLITICAL COMMENTATOR

APRIL 4

Today, the demand that everyone listen and be listened to is the hope of an endangered but potentially self-healing world.

MARGARET MEAD, ANTHROPOLOGIST

APRIL 5

All human beings are our allies; we must respect the lives of every-one on the planet and maintain deep concern for their well-being. When we care for each other, we are no longer afraid.

LEONARDO BOFF, LIBERATION THEOLOGIAN

APRIL 6

*I*t is not only participation in the material gains and freedom which are being demanded by the world's people – but also the dignity of sharing in all decisions that affect a person's own life or that of his or her kin and neighbors, descendants, and successors. And, with the demand for participation will come, inevitably, contribution *from* each *to* the whole.

MARGARET MEAD, ANTHROPOLOGIST

APRIL 7

*T*hrough our scientific and technological genius, we have made of this world a neighborhood and yet . . . we have not had the ethical commitment to make it a brotherhood. But somehow, and in some way, we have got to do this. We must all learn to live together as brothers or we will perish together as fools. We are tied together in this single garment of destiny, caught in an inescapable network of mutuality.

MARTIN LUTHER KING, JR., CIVIL RIGHTS LEADER

APRIL 8

*F*ull peace and full democracy – peace and democracy that are healthy enough to last – both involve the simultaneous co-creation of our individual and collective well-being.

TOM ATLEE, FOUNDER, CO-INTELLIGENCE INSTITUTE

APRIL 9

*W*e are learning that joy is still available, not from the circumstances, but from our relationships. As long as we're together, as long as we feel others supporting us, we persevere.

MARGARET WHEATLEY, CORPORATE CONSULTANT

APRIL 10

*Y*ou gradually struggle less and less for an idea and more and more for specific people . . . in the end, it is the reality of personal relationship that saves everything.

THOMAS MERTON, MONASTIC

APRIL 11

*U*p there you go around every hour and a half, time after time after time. You look down there and you can't imagine how many borders and boundaries you cross, again and again and again, and you don't even see them. When you go around the Earth in an hour and half, you begin to recognize that your identity is with the whole thing. And that makes a change. And from where you see it . . . the earth is a whole, and it's so beautiful. You wish you could take a person in each hand, one from each side in the various conflicts, and say, "Look. Look at it from this perspective. Look at that. What's important?"

RUSTY SCHWEICKART, ASTRONAUT

APRIL 12

*M*y mother told me, "It doesn't matter if we came on the Mayflower, a slave ship, across the Rio Grande or through Ellis Island. Now we are all in this boat together."

CAROL MOSELY BRAUN, US SENATOR

APRIL 13

*G*iven certain circumstances and the liberty to try, ordinary people will consistently do extraordinary things.

DEE HOCK, FOUNDER, VISA INTERNATIONAL

APRIL 14

*P*eople are people – strike them, and they will cry; cut them and they will bleed; starve them, and they will wither away and die. But treat them with respect and decency, give them equal access to the levers of power, attend to their aspirations and grievances, and they will flourish and grow and, if you will excuse an ungrammatical phrase, join together "to form a more perfect Union."

THURGOOD MARSHALL, JUSTICE, US SUPREME COURT

APRIL 15

I am a citizen, not of Athens nor of Greece, but of the whole world. The world is my parish.

SOCRATES, PHILOSOPHER

APRIL 16

I do not believe that oppression anywhere or injustice which is tolerated by people of any country toward any group in that country is a healthy influence. I feel that unless we learn to live together as individuals and as groups, and to find ways of settling our difficulties without showing fear of each other and resorting to force, we cannot hope to see our democracy successful.

ELEANOR ROOSEVELT, A CO-AUTHOR OF
UNIVERSAL DECLARATION OF HUMAN RIGHTS

APRIL 17

We declare that this Republic can only endure as a free government while built upon the love of the people for each other and for the nation; that it cannot be pinned together by bayonets; that the Civil War is over, and that every passion and resentment which grew out of it must die with it, and that we must be in fact, as we are in name, one united brotherhood of free men.

POPULIST PARTY PLATFORM, 1892

APRIL 18

Not like the brazen giant of Greek fame,
With conquering limbs astride from land to land;
Here at our sea-washed, sunset gates shall stand
A mighty woman with a torch, whose flame
Is the imprisoned lightning, and her name
Mother of Exiles. From her beacon-hand
Glows worldwide welcome; her mild eyes command
The air-bridged harbor that twin cities frame.
"Keep, ancient lands, your storied pomp!" cries she
With silent lips. "Give me your tired, your poor,
Your huddled masses yearning to breathe free,
The wretched refuse of your teeming shore.
Send these, the homeless, tempest-tost to me,
I lift my lamp beside the golden door!"

EMMA LAZARUS, POET

APRIL 19

My country is the world. My countrymen are mankind.

THOMAS PAINE, STATESMAN

APRIL 20

I pledge allegiance to compassion, humility and integrity and to the United States of America . . . One diverse nation under many beliefs with liberty and justice for all.

A 21ST-CENTURY PLEDGE OF ALLEGIANCE
JERRIN ZUMBERG, YOUNG DEMOCRATIC VISIONARY

APRIL 21

Wisdom Council Story

W e are a group of local citizens who are working to bring Wisdom Councils to Oregon. Wisdom Councils empower citizens and enhance the vitality of democracy. Four times a year, citizens are randomly selected to form a Wisdom Council and to represent "the people." We meet on two successive days. A facilitator helps us express our thoughts and arrive at consensual statements. Immediately after we meet, we present our conclusions to an assembled audience and on community TV. In this meeting, everyone listens to the panel's consensual statements and forms into small groups to discuss them. The presentation is videotaped and made available to the community.

Most people experience politics as an adversarial process. Many people have never had an experience of being in a creative political conversation, where people seek win/win solutions that may go beyond the ideas offered by politicians. The Wisdom Council shows people that creative political conversations are possible by including them in one.

ROGUE VALLEY WISDOM COUNCIL, ASHLAND OREGON

APRIL 22

*Y*ou have to trust people's ability to develop their capacity for working collectively to solve problems.

MYLES HORTON, FOUNDER, HIGHLANDER SCHOOL

APRIL 23

I celebrate myself and sing myself
And what I assume
you shall assume.
For every atom belonging
to me as good belongs to you.

WALT WHITMAN, POET AND WRITER

APRIL 24

*W*e cannot be silent. In the process of our growing democracy, the people's opinion gains power and range. Everything happening on this earth applies to all of us. Only by uniting our efforts . . . will we help ourselves survive in this still green world.

ASSEMBLY OF 5000 PEOPLE, KAZAKHSTAN

APRIL 25

*T*he gathering included indigenous people, African Americans, Asian Americans, Latinos, and European Americans; artists, corporate consultants, community activists, entertainers, ministers, political representatives, and labor organizers; Christians, Buddhists, Jews, Muslims, pagans and persons who are simply spiritual; youth and elders, gays and straights. The only characteristic these people shared was a history of extraordinary dedication to the common good.

ROBERTO VARGAS, COMMUNITY ACTIVIST

APRIL 26

*D*emocracy is faith in humanity, not faith in "poor" people or "ignorant" people, but faith in every living soul . . . champions of democracy are not looking down to raise anyone up, they recognize that all [people] must face one another squarely with the knowledge that the give and take between them is equal.

MARY PARKER FOLLETT, VISIONARY

APRIL 27

*F*aith in others does a lot of work. It doesn't mean blind faith – observing helplessly while keeping your fingers crossed – it means to remain alert to what's going on, and then to fill another with the strength of your faith to such an extent that they feel able to do whatever needs to be done.

DADI JANKI, SPIRITUAL TEACHER

*W*e shall work to build new relationships with each other, between men and women, between producers and consumers, between urban and rural, between North and South, between human beings and nature. These processes of democratization at all levels, will be exercised by alliances of people throughout the world – Alliances of Hope – which will be formed in dynamic interaction in the spirit of peace, tolerance, ecological sanity, and peaceful coexistence. People's governance will be rooted in these alliances.

SAGARMATHA DECLARATION, KATHMANDU

APRIL 29

*I*f civilizations are to survive, we must cultivate the sciences of human relationships – the ability of all people, of all kinds, to live together and work together in the same world at peace. The only limit to our realization of tomorrow will be our doubts of today.

FRANKLIN DELANO ROOSEVELT, US PRESIDENT, 1933-1945

APRIL 30

My fellow citizens of the world: ask not what America will do for you, but what together we can do for the freedom of man.

JOHN FITZGERALD KENNEDY, US PRESIDENT, 1961-1963

M A Y

Interdependence

Interdependence evokes images of networks — "a web of connections among equals" — observed the late ecologist Donella Meadows. Our very lives depend upon the coherence of interconnecting networks of our fellow beings living in accord with nature. We are at our best when we act out of a deep understanding that we are but one part of a globally interdependent web of life. When we truly understand that we cannot — and should not — be isolated from the effects of our actions, we begin to make wise choices. When we release the illusion of separateness and let go of the conceit of independent action we begin to make wise choices. A greater democracy is like a vibrant meadow. All the inhabitants thrive in the interconnected web.

M AY 1

*O*ne has but to observe a community of beavers at work in a stream to understand the loss in his sagacity, balance, cooperation, competence, and purpose which Man has suffered since he rose up on his hind legs. . . . He began to chatter and he developed Reason, Thought, and Imagination, qualities which would get the smartest group of rabbits or orioles in the world into inextricable trouble overnight.

JAMES THURBER, AUTHOR

M AY 2

*C*onclusions arrived at through reasoning have very little or no influence in altering the course of our lives.

CARLOS CASTANEDA, AUTHOR

M AY 3

*W*hen will we learn, when will the people of the world get up and say, enough is enough. God created us for fellowship. God created us so that we should form the human family, existing together because we were made for one another. We are not made for an exclusive self-sufficiency but for interdependence, and we break the law of our being at our peril.

DESMOND TUTU, ANGLICAN BISHOP

MAY 4

When we try and pick out anything by itself, we find it hitched to everything in the universe.

JOHN MUIR, ENVIRONMENTALIST

MAY 5

The earth is what we all have in common. It is what we are made of and what we live from, and we cannot damage it without damaging those with whom we share it. There is an uncanny resemblance between our behavior toward each other and our behavior toward the earth. By some connection we do not recognize, the willingness to exploit one becomes the willingness to exploit the other. . . . It is impossible to care for each other more or differently than we care for the earth.

WENDELL BERRY, POET

MAY 6

*A*mericans will never find true peace until they come into harmony with the place where they live.

CARL JUNG, PSYCHOLOGIST

MAY 7

*E*very nation must now develop an overriding loyalty to mankind as a whole in order to preserve the best in their individual societies.

MARTIN LUTHER KING, JR., CIVIL RIGHTS ACTIVIST

MAY 8

*T*he universe bends to life and you and I are proof. The core principle of how life has succeeded is that it is interdependent. Ants know that. Bees know that. People know that. The hours of the day that we spend in cooperation with other people far exceed the number of hours we spend killing people.

JAMES HIGHTOWER, AUTHOR

MAY 9

*O*ur lives extend beyond our skins, in radical interdependence with the rest of the world.

JOANNA MACY, BUDDHIST SCHOLAR AND ECO-PHILOSOPHER

MAY 10

*W*e are united with all life that is in nature. Man no longer lives his life for himself alone.

ALBERT SCHWEITZER, HUMANITARIAN

MAY 11

*A*chain is as strong as its weakest link. Strong ones will see to it that weaker ones get stronger. To be a servant of others is a high role.

ROY LITTLESUN, TEACHER HOPI TRADITION

MAY 12

I wonder whether you realize a deep, great fact. That souls, all human souls, are interconnected . . . that we can not only pray for each other but suffer for each other. Nothing is more real than this interconnection – this precious power put by God into the very heart of our infirmities.

FRIEDRICH VON HUGEL, THEOLOGIAN

MAY 13

*H*umans have become so numerous and our tools so powerful that we have driven fellow creatures to extinction, dammed the great rivers, torn down ancient forests, poisoned the earth, rain and wind, and ripped holes in the sky. Our science has brought pain as well as joy; our comfort is paid for by the suffering of millions. We are learning from our mistakes, we are mourning our vanished kin, and we now build a new politics of hope.

DECLARATION OF INTERDEPENDENCE,
DAVID SUZUKI FOUNDATION TEAM,
EARTH SUMMIT 1994

MAY 14

When we think we're separate, we lose power. Whenever I say "my," I have lost my power. Power is not my power; it is not enlarging oneself as a separate individual. It is only gainable as part of a larger whole. Whenever you shut down connectedness, you get depressed.

GLENDA TAYLOR, ARTIST

MAY 15

When in the course of human events it becomes necessary for the people of a metropolitan area to recognize the importance of the economic, cultural, and natural ties that connect them to one another, a deep respect for the opinions of its citizens requires that they should declare the causes which impel them to proclaim their interdependence.

We hold these truths to be self evident . . . that we all prosper or decline together, that we all breathe the same air and drink the same water, and that we all are part of one society that cannot be allowed to fragment into isolated pieces . . . to these ends it is imperative to institute reforms and new coalitions, laying their foundation on such principles as shall better effect competitiveness, sustainability, and fairness.

REGIONAL PLAN ASSOCIATION, A REGION AT RISK: THE THIRD REGIONAL PLAN FOR THE NEW YORK-NEW JERSEY-CONNECTICUT METROPOLITAN AREA

MAY 16

I am only a small spark.
Let me ignite something.
Something that burns hot and true,
Through illusion and destructiveness.
Let the light of that fire illuminate
Suddenly the web of interrelatedness,
The sureness of consequences,
The extent of time,
The preciousness of things here,
So that the mind receiving this vision
Is ecstatic and self-aware
And loves the world enough
To be more careful. This is enough.

JORDON FISHER-SMITH, FOREST RANGER AND AUTHOR

MAY 17

We, the citizens and institutions of Bloomington and Monroe County Indiana, make this declaration of our interdependence and mutual aspirations.

We believe a preschool through postsecondary educational system focused on students learning will achieve a literate, thoughtful and effective citizenry and is the critical ingredient of a healthy, competitive global economy and a viable multicultural democracy . . .

CITIZENS, BLOOMINGTON, INDIANA

MAY 18

o feel the love of people whom we know is a fire that feeds our life. But to feel the affection that comes from those we do not know – that is something still greater and more beautiful because it widens out the boundaries of our being and unites all living things.

PABLO NERUDA, POET

MAY 19

hen the lead goose gets tired, it rotates back into formation, and another goose flies at the point position. Lesson: It pays to take turns doing the hard tasks and sharing leadership with people: as with geese, we are interdependent on each other.

MILTON OLSEN, AUTHOR

MAY 20

emocracy in its simplest form of sharing power, listening, and gathering information, is the only sustainable form of governing ourselves, because no one likes being told what to do by others.

ARNOLD MINDELL, PSYCHOLOGIST AND WRITER

MAY 21

That I cannot now predict your future is exactly what makes mine unpredictable. Our futures enter into each other. What is your future, and mine, become ours. We prepare each other for surprise.

JAMES P. CARSE, AUTHOR

MAY 22

The story of the 20th century was finding out just how big and powerful we were. And it turns out that we're big and powerful as all get out. The story of the 21st century is going to be finding out ways to get smaller or not. To see if we can summon the will, and then the way, to make ourselves somewhat smaller, and try to fit back into this planet.

BILL McKIBBON, AUTHOR

MAY 23

Through kindness, through affection, through honesty, through truth and justice toward all others we ensure our own benefit.

H.H. DALAI LAMA, SPIRITUAL LEADER

MAY 24

The important lesson to realize is that we are all made of the same fabric, we're part of the same web.

DR. VICTORIA ELIZABETH FOE, BIOLOGIST

MAY 25

The cause of all violence is the inability of people to deal with difference constructively.

MOHAMMED ABU-NIMER, PROFESSOR, PEACE STUDIES

MAY 26

A network is nonhierarchical. It is a web of connections among equals. What holds it together is not force, obligation, material incentive, or social contract, but rather shared values and the understanding that some tasks can be accomplished together that could never be accomplished separately. One of the important purposes of a network is simply to remind its members that they are not alone.

DONELLA H. MEADOWS, SYSTEMS ANALYST AND FARMER

MAY 27

*N*one of us can expect to act on more than a tiny corner of the great complexity. But in our interrelated society, itself part of an uncompromisingly interdependent world, we have to think about the whole complexity in order to act relevantly on any part of it.

HARLAN CLEVELAND, PUBLIC EXECUTIVE AND VISIONARY

MAY 28

Earth Home

*S*haron and Pat, two Catholic sisters, created a urban garden and when they did, they reclaimed a neighborhood that was once torn by violence and despair. At first, they planted "sunflower trees", cherry tomatoes and vegetables and offered them to neighborhood children in exchange for their help in the garden. Pat explains, "what happened is that the earth became the place where people in the neighborhood could meet around common interests." Soon children and adult neighbors were coming in regularly to help in the garden. Pat and Sharon reflect, "from the earth we learned the spirit of cooperation, a different way than violence to solve differences."

SHARON JOYER AND PAT NAGLE, URBAN GARDENERS

MAY 29

What we desperately need is a global acknowledgment of the fact that no people and no nation can truly prosper unless the bounty of our collective ingenuity and opportunities are available and accessible to all. . . . In the wake of Sept. 11 this is not idle or naïve rhetoric, but rather a matter of survival.

WADE DAVIS, EXPLORER-IN-RESIDENCE, NATIONAL GEOGRAPHIC

MAY 30

If I am to eliminate my own sufferings, I must act in the knowledge that I exist in dependent relationships with other human beings and the whole of nature.

H.H. DALAI LAMA, SPIRITUAL LEADER

MAY 31

Success is the gathering together of all that is beautiful.

RALPH WALDO EMERSON, POET AND WRITER

JUNE

Emergence

Have you watched how ants organize themselves? How bees work to make a beehive? Or, how beavers manage to create underwater dens? What usually looks like relatively simple interconnected tasks results in a complex habitat that nourishes and sustains life for these creatures. This phenomenon of interconnected creativity that gives rise to a higher order is called "emergence." Human beings participate in this kind of emergent system too. From relatively simple yet interconnected behaviors, people create supportive structures and organizations. For example, the willingness to trust and to be trustworthy is one elemental human behavior that results in deeply democratic organizations.

We are yearning for supportive structures: families, neighborhoods, communities, organizations and institutions that satisfy our needs and that are in harmony with nature. We also actively participate in the emergence of these kinds of structures everyday.

J U N E 1

*T*think the Constitution is one of the great documents in the world. How has it survived two hundred years? Because it is not what it was. We ought to look at the Constitution through its metamorphosis – from a document that denied the personhood of black people and denied the political reality of women, to a document that has, in part, through war and struggle, come to encompass them and others.

ELEANOR HOLMES NORTON, CIVIL RIGHTS ATTORNEY

J U N E 2

*A*merica, you've never been America to me: and I swear this oath someday you will be!

LANGSTON HUGHES, POET

J U N E 3

*T*t is, in fact, our imperfections that most unite us and make of us a social organism whose parts are busy assisting one another.

MATHEW FOX, THEOLOGIAN

JUNE 4

A community gradually discovers as it grows that it is not simply for itself. It belongs to humanity. It has received a gift which must bear fruit for all people. If it closes in on itself, it will suffocate. When it begins, a community is like a seed which must grow to become a tree which will give abundant fruit, in which the birds of the air can make their nests. It must open its arms wide, and hold out its hands to give freely what it has freely received.

A community must always remember that it is a sign and a witness for all people. Its members must be faithful to each other if they are to grow. But they must also be faithful as a sign and source of hope for all humankind.

JEAN VANIER, AUTHOR

JUNE 5

T he familiar life horizon has been outgrown, the old concepts, ideals and emotional patterns no longer fit; the time for the passing of a threshold is at hand.

JOSEPH CAMPBELL, MYTHOLOGIST

JUNE 6

I don't give a fig for simplicity on this side of complexity, but I would give my life for simplicity on the other side.

OLIVER WENDELL HOLMES, JR., US SUPREME COURT JUSTICE

JUNE 7

*P*lanetary democracy does not yet exist but our global civilization is already preparing a place for it. It is the very Earth we inhabit, linked with Heaven above us. Only in this setting can the mutuality and the commonality of the human race be newly created with reverence and gratitude for that which transcends each of us and all of us together.

VACLAV HAVEL, PRESIDENT, CZECH REPUBLIC, 1993-2003

JUNE 8

*T*he whole life of an individual is nothing more but the process of giving birth to himself, indeed we should be fully born when we die.

ERICH FROMM, PSYCHOLOGIST

*I*t is historically and biologically true that there can be no growth without birth and growing pains. Whenever there is emergence of the new we confront the recalcitrance of the old. So the tensions which we witness in the world today are indicative of the fact that a new world order is being born and an old one is passing away.

MARTIN LUTHER KING, JR., CIVIL RIGHTS LEADER

JUNE 10

Divine Creator, President of the Universe,
Chief Executive of Planets, Stars, and Galaxies!
Thy democratic rule, giving the rights of free will and self-
     evolution to thy citizen children is bringing them nearer
     and nearer to Thine ideals.

PARAMAHANSA YOGANANDA, SPIRITUAL LEADER

JUNE 11

*A*t the boundary, life blossoms.

JAMES GLEICK, SCIENCE WRITER

JUNE 12

*A*n invasion of armies can be resisted, but not an idea whose time has come.

VICTOR HUGO, AUTHOR

JUNE 13

I think our species is evolving from homo sapiens to homo spiritus.

ROBERT BOISSIERE, AUTHOR AND TEACHER

JUNE 14

*I*t is an escape for persons to cry, when this question of the equality of people is raised, . . . "Ah, but the situation is not so simple." . . . No great stride is ever made for the individual or for the human race unless the complex situation is reduced to one simple question and its simple answer.

PEARL S. BUCK, AUTHOR

JUNE 15

*M*ost of us spend too much time on the last twenty-four hours and too little on the last six thousand years.

WILL DURANT, HISTORIAN

JUNE 16

*T*he notion of progress in a single line without goal or limit seems perhaps the most parochial notion of a very parochial century.

LEWIS MUMFORD, EDUCATOR

JUNE 17

*Y*ou can't say that civilization doesn't advance . . . for in every war they kill you a new way.

WILL ROGERS, HUMORIST

JUNE 18

*S*imple, clear purpose and principles give rise to complex and intelligent behavior. Complex rules and regulations give rise to simple and stupid behavior.

DEE HOCK, FOUNDER, VISA INTERNATIONAL

JUNE 19

*T*he universe in its emergence is neither determined nor random, but creative.

THEODOSIUS DOBZHANSKY, GENETICIST

JUNE 20

The enormous creative forces deep in the reality of things are asserting themselves.

THOMAS BERRY, ECOLOGIST AND THEOLOGIAN

JUNE 21

A process which led from the amoeba to man appeared to philosophers to be obviously progress – though whether the amoeba would agree with this opinion is not known.

BERTRAND RUSSELL, PHILOSOPHER

JUNE 22

The caterpillar does all the work and the butterfly gets all the publicity.

GEORGE CARLIN, COMEDIAN

JUNE 23

When the forms of the old culture are dying, the new culture is created by a few people who are not afraid to be insecure.

RUDOLF BAHRO, SOCIALIST

JUNE 24

They can crush all the roses they want to, but they will not be able to postpone the spring.

OCTAVIO PAZ, POET

JUNE 25

Emergent democracy is about leadership through giving up control, activating the people to engage through deliberation and action, and allowing emergent order to grow from the grass roots.

JOICHI ITO, INTERNET ENTREPRENEUR

JUNE 26

*S*elf-similarity is achieved not through compliance to an exhausting set of standards and rules, but from a few simple principles that everyone is accountable for, operating in a condition of individual freedom.

MARGARET WHEATLEY, CORPORATE CONSULTANT

JUNE 27

*I*n moments of confusion such as the present, we are not left simply with our own rational contrivances. We are supported by the ultimate powers of the universe as they make themselves present to us through the spontaneities within our own being.

THOMAS BERRY, ECOLOGIST AND THEOLOGIAN

JUNE 28

*L*ocal information can lead to global wisdom.

STEVEN JOHNSON, AUTHOR

JUNE 29

Look to the ant, thou sluggard;
Consider her ways be wise:
Which having no chief, overseer, or ruler,
Provides her meat in the summer,
And gathers her food in the harvest.

PROVERBS 6:6-8

JUNE 30

*E*mergence, to a great degree, is simply what we didn't plan. How to arrive at the best possible unplanned outcome is what emergent democracy is about.

MITCH RATCLIFFE, AUTHOR

JULY

Creativity

People create — it is what we do. Creativity evolves from our own thoughts and imagination — it brings something new into being. It is irrepressible. Human creativity and resourcefulness are untapped sources of renewable energy and power. The genius of a true democracy is that it frees the creative human spirit and utilizes this power for the good of all.

Given insurmountable odds, people continually create workable solutions. Given despair and loss, people recreate their lives. Given uncertainty, fear, dislocation and violence, people create exquisite art, acts of compassion, and renewed relationships. We tend to think that real power resides in military and corporate control — but authentic power rests in the relentless creative spirit of humanity. The pulse of a greater democracy is the creative power of people.

JULY 1

*W*hen the creative power that depends on no one else is aroused, there is a release of energy, simplicity, enthusiasm. The word enthusiasm is Greek for "filled with theos" filled with God.

STEPHEN NACHMANOVITCH, MUSICIAN AND AUTHOR

JULY 2

*C*reativity is a type of learning process where the teacher and the pupil are located in the same individual.

ARTHUR KOESTLER, NOVELIST

JULY 3

*A*nd so some of us are taking responsibility now to envision and create the democracy we want . . . to create our world again . . . The better democracy we will create will give ultimate power back to We the People while at the same time ensuring that wiser decisions emerge from our citizenship and the work of our representatives.

TOM ATLEE, FOUNDER, CO-INTELLIGENCE INSTITUTE

July 4

Let the people explode into this new millennium with the exhilaration of being true to the glory of this democracy.

THE CONTENDER, HOLLYWOOD FILM

July 5

The Constitution is the greatest improvisational document ever created. Written on four pieces of parchment at the end of the 18th century, it is still able to adjust to the thorniest problems of the fledgling 21st. It sets us on our improvisational course, emphasizing that we are a nation in the process of becoming.

KEN BURNS, AUTHOR

July 6

Jazz music begins to explain to you what it means to be an American. Which is that it's a process. And democracy is a process. . . . Jazz believes in freedom of expression. But it also believes in people communicating with each other. . . . You have eight musicians and . . . there's written music but then you leave that score and are left to make intelligent decisions – decisions that have soul. Decisions that allow your personality to breathe and to speak, but decisions that allow for others people's personalities to breathe, too. . . . You are always negotiating . . . and so you have that question of integrity, the intent, the will to play together. That is what jazz music is. So you have yourself, your individual expression – then you have to figure out how to fit in with everybody else. And that's exactly like democracy.

WYNTON MARSALIS, MUSICIAN

July 7

[It is necessary] to do the right thing because the heart and mind have been touched and because it is the only logical thing to do, popular opinion not withstanding.

WANGARI MAATHAI, ENVIRONMENTALIST

JULY 8

Let us be realists, let us do the impossible.

ERNESTO "CHE" GUEVARA, REVOLUTIONARY

JULY 9

Citizenship means that I act as if this larger place were mine to create, while the conventional wisdom is that I cannot have responsibility without authority. That is a tired idea. Let it die in peace. I am responsible for the health of the institution and the community even though I do not control it. I can participate in creating something I do not control.

PETER BLOCK, AUTHOR

JULY 10

We have it in our power to begin the world all over again. A situation similar to the present hath not appeared since the days of Noah until now. The birthday of a new world is at hand.

THOMAS PAINE, STATESMAN

JULY 11

The things we fear most in organizations . . . fluctuations, disturbances, imbalances – are the primary sources of creativity.

MARGARET WHEATLEY, CORPORATE CONSULTANT

JULY 12

Living is a form of not being sure, not knowing what's next or how. The moment you know how, you begin to die a little. The artist never entirely knows – we guess – we may be wrong, but we take leap after leap into the dark.

AGNES DE MILLE, CHOREOGRAPHER

JULY 13

We lay there and looked up at the night sky and she told me about the stars called blue squares and red swirls and I told her I'd never heard of them. Of course not, she said the really important stuff they never tell you. You have to imagine it on your own.

BRIAN ANDREAS, ARTIST

July 14

Only think: if all our imaginative resources currently employed in inventing new power games and bigger and better weaponry were reoriented toward disarmament, what miracles we could achieve, what new truths, what undiscovered realms of beauty.

LEONARD BERNSTEIN, CONDUCTOR

July 15

Perhaps life itself seems lunatic, who knows where madness lies. Perhaps to be too practical is madness. To surrender to dreams – this may be madness. To seek treasures where there is only trash. Too much sanity may be madness. And maddest of all, to see life as it is and not as it should be.

MIGUEL DE CERVANTES, AUTHOR

July 16

The art of progress is to preserve order amid change, and to preserve change amid order.

ALFRED NORTH WHITEHEAD, MATHEMATICIAN AND PHILOSOPHER

July 17

*T*he thing about democracy, beloved, is that it is not neat, orderly, or quiet. It requires a certain relish for confusion.

MOLLY IVINS, COLUMNIST

July 18

*T*ell me what it is you plan to do with your one wild and precious life?

MARY OLIVER, POET

July 19

We hold these truths to be self-evident;
All people are born creative;
Endowed by our creator
With the inalienable right and responsibility
To express our creativity
For the sake of ourselves and our world.

BARBARA MARX HUBBARD, FUTURIST

July 20

You know sometimes it is the artist's task to find out how much music you can still make with what you have left.

ITZHAK PERLMAN, VIOLINIST

July 21

Artful Service

As a service project to celebrate his bar mitzvah, Kevin organized an art show for Sara and Bilquis, two young Muslim refugees from Afghanistan living in Houston. He wanted to sell their paintings to raise money for their family

Every one of the paintings sold. I watched as people shared the experiences of this selfless act of one. I saw Muslims, Jews, Christians . . . and others, eat together, talk together, pray together. As musicians played music that celebrated arts and diversity, I saw brothers and sisters in my fellow humans. One of the musicians summed it up best, "Art presents us with the paradox that no matter how different our expressions we all need to communicate and create." . . . Today is a challenge for all of us to dig deep into our own personal form of creativity and imagine how we can use it to be a positive force in the world.

P.K. McCRARY, STORYTELLER

July 22

A major activity of a democratic community is developing the skills, procedures, and attitudes needed for people to jointly create with their diversity. As more people become artists with these democratic tools, the community's thinking becomes more wise, their collective behavior more intelligent and successful.

TOM ATLEE, FOUNDER, CO-INTELLIGENCE INSTITUTE

July 23

T he creative process is a spiritual path. This adventure is about us, about the deep self, the composer in all of us, about originality, meaning not that which is all new, but that which is fully and originally ourselves.

STEPHEN NACHMANOVITCH, MUSICIAN AND AUTHOR

July 24

*D*emocracy – a political system based on dignity and freedom in which the people rule, a vision of people having control over the basic issues that affect their lives from political decisions, to economic factors to the state of the world we hand off to our children.

PATRICK REINSBOROUGH, AUTHOR

July 25

*W*e do not get the whole power of the group unless every individual is given full value, is giving full value. It is the creative spontaneity of each which makes life march on. . . . The doctrine of true democracy is that every man (and woman) is and must be a creative citizen.

MARY PARKER FOLLETT, VISIONARY

July 26

*D*emocracy is like sex. When it is good it is great and when it is bad, it is still pretty good.

GARRISON KEILLOR, HUMORIST AND AUTHOR

JULY 27

*H*ear me! Allow yourself the conceit to believe that the flame of democracy will never go out as long as there is one candle in your hand.

BILL MOYERS, JOURNALIST

JULY 28

I have a dream of children so bold and yet caring,
of strangers so kind and yet compassionate,
of good parents so gentle yet wise,
of good generals so peaceful yet creative,

. . . oooh where could we go if we took a ride on this dream
forever?
. . . just whisper that sweet name and believe in it

you'll hear democracy
they'll hear democracy
the children will listen and hear democracy –
everyone will listen and believe.

ANONYMOUS

J u l y   2 9

We are not permitted to choose the frame of our destiny but what we put into it is ours.

DAG HAMMARSKJOLD, SECRETARY-GENERAL UNITED NATIONS

J u l y   3 0

The word creative is among the most mysterious words in any language. As with our words in general, this word has been trivialized. Its numinous and magical qualities have been diminished – also its visionary quality.

THOMAS BERRY, ECOLOGIST AND THEOLOGIAN

J u l y   3 1

Let the beauty we love, be what we do. There are hundreds of ways to kneel and bless the ground.

RUMI, POET

A U G U S T

Spirit Within

In a poem, Wendell Berry says, "be joyful though you have considered all of the facts." Spirit within is a source of renewable joy for us no matter what the exterior circumstances are. Spirit within, by whatever name or experience we call it, is our wellspring when the going gets tough. Inner life with spirit is not a holy retreat from life's difficulty, but it is our comfort, strength, and joy in the midst of life.

Active citizens meeting the inevitable suffering and struggles of life in a greater democracy are called to harness this inner spirit, this divine sweet and fiery force inside us, and give it to others through our convictions, efforts, and participation. People of spirit convey that it is possible for people like us to make real the principles of a greater democracy. Hope, trust, and renewable joy, the gifts of the spirit within, are ours.

AUGUST 1

*A*lthough attempting to bring about world peace through the internal transformation of individuals is difficult, it is the only way.

THICH NHAT HANH, SPIRITUAL TEACHER

AUGUST 2

*T*here is a vitality, a life force, an energy, a quickening that is translated through you into action and because there is only one of you in all time, its expression is unique. And, if you block it, it will never exist through any other medium and will be lost.

MARTHA GRAHAM, DANCER

AUGUST 3

*T*he spirit we have not the work we do makes us important to the people around us.

SISTER JOAN CHITTISTER, SPIRITUAL TEACHER

AUGUST 4

I believe in democracy because it releases the energy of every human being.

WOODROW WILSON, US PRESIDENT, 1913-1921

AUGUST 5

*L*iberty lies in the hearts of men and women; when it dies there, no constitution, no law, no court can save it.

LEARNED HAND, JUSTICE, US SUPREME COURT

AUGUST 6

*W*e are children of men who have not been afraid of new continents or new ideas. In our blood is the impulse to leap to the highest we can see, as the wills of our fathers fixed themselves on the convictions of their hearts. To spring forward and then to follow the path steadfastly is forever the duty of Americans. We must live democracy.

MARY PARKER FOLLETT, VISIONARY

August 7

*W*hile wagon trains rolled west in the 19th century, others stayed east and traveled further in their minds than any horse could take them. The aspiration to a better life had an inner as well as an outer direction, and this impulse, founded on the urge for the good and the true, has always been at the heart of what America stands for.

ROGER HOUSDEN, AUTHOR

August 8

*T*here are within each of us god-given talents that do not respond to market pressures, yet spring to life in the presence of honor and respect. The spirit within compels us to serve each other rather than condemn each other and place our primary attention on the extension of brotherly love.

MARIANNE WILLIAMSON, AUTHOR

A U G U S T 9

Touching One Life is Great, Too

*W*hen I was two my father died, my mother was killed when I was six. I moved in with my grandma, who died when I was nine. I have since been adopted, and all my pains, I believe, have made me a stronger person. Listening to Mairead Corrigan Maguire (Nobel peace laureate), I realized I did not have to sit and watch the world die. I am going to touch people's lives. Probably not anything as great as Mairead had done, but like she said, touching one person's life is great, too. I'm planning on volunteering in a nursing home and listening to their ideas of peace, and just getting to know them and show my respect for the forgotten members of our community.

SARAH JOHNSON, 10TH-GRADE STUDENT

A U G U S T 10

I built a building of light in the worst part of Pittsburgh to be a light in the neighborhood. My idea was to build it where there was no sunlight and where the cancer of poverty was at its worst. It was a vocational school for steelworkers, welfare mothers, unemployed people who were retraining for new lives. I got the best to teach poor people so that they knew they had value. They needed to be reminded of their dreams.

BILL STRICKLAND, EDUCATOR

AUGUST 11

A man should learn to detect and watch that gleam of light which flashes across his mind from within, more than the luster of the firmament of bards and sages.

RALPH WALDO EMERSON, POET AND WRITER

AUGUST 12

Never give up,
No matter what is going on
Never give up
Develop the heart.
Too much energy in your country
is spent developing the mind
instead of the heart.
Be compassionate
and I say again
Never give up
No matter what is happening
No matter what is going on around you
Never give up.

H.H. DALAI LAMA, SPIRITUAL LEADER

AUGUST 13

*L*ife will either grind you down or polish you up. And which it does is your choice.

ROGER WALSH, AUTHOR

AUGUST 14

*W*ith the fearful strain on me night and day, if I did not laugh I should die.

ABRAHAM LINCOLN, US PRESIDENT, 1861-1865

AUGUST 15

*L*augh and grow strong.

ST. IGNATIUS OF LOYOLA

AUGUST 16

*T*he quest for democracy . . . is part of the unceasing human endeavor to prove that the spirit of man can transcend the flaws of his nature.

AUNG SUNG SUU KYI, PRO-DEMOCRACY ACTIVIST

AUGUST 17

*W*e fully trust the human spirit. We believe in its beauty and its courage.

GITA BROOKE, INTERNATIONAL PEACE NETWORKER

AUGUST 18

*W*hen I despair I remember that all through history the way of truth and love have always won. There have been tyrants and murderers and for a time they seem invincible, but in the end they always fail. Think of it, always.

MAHATMA GANDHI, SPIRITUAL AND POLITICAL LEADER

AUGUST 19

The blanket of fear was lifted by Negro youth. When they took their struggle to the streets, a new spirit of resistance was born. Inspired by the boldness of and the ingenuity of Negroes, white youth stirred into action and formed an alliance that aroused the conscience of a nation.

MARTIN LUTHER KING, JR., CIVIL RIGHTS LEADER

AUGUST 20

When you do things from your soul, you feel a river moving in you, a joy. When actions come from another section, the feeling disappears.

RUMI, POET

AUGUST 21

Wherever you are is the entry point.

KABIR, POET

AUGUST 22

The Universe is evolving towards an even greater destiny, and we are the means of this global transformation.

PIR VILAYAT INAYAT KHAN, SPIRITUAL TEACHER

AUGUST 23

The place to touch the Kingdom of God is within us. We do not have to die to arrive at the gate of Heaven. In fact, we have to truly be alive. If we touch deeply enough, the Kingdom of God will become a reality here and now. This is not a matter of devotion. It is a matter of practice.

THICH NHAT HANH, SPIRITUAL TEACHER

AUGUST 24

Somehow or other human beings must get a feeling that there is in life a spring, a spring which flows for all humanity, perhaps like the old legendary spring from which men drew eternal youth. This spring must fortify the soul and give the people a vital reason for wanting to meet the problems of the world today, and to meet them in a way which will make life more worth living for everyone. It must be a source of inspiration and faith.

ELEANOR ROOSEVELT, A CO-AUTHOR OF
UNIVERSAL DECLARATION OF HUMAN RIGHTS

A U G U S T   2 5

*T*he great paradox of the 21st century is that, in this age of powerful technology, the biggest problems we face internationally are problems of the human soul.

RALPH PETERS, U.S. ARMY LIEUTENANT COLONEL

A U G U S T   2 6

I am of the opinion that my life belongs to the whole community, and as long as I live, it is my privilege to do for it whatever I can. I want to be thoroughly used up when I die, for the harder I work, the more I live. I rejoice in life for its own sake. Life is no brief candle to me, it is sort of a splendid torch which I've got a hold of for the moment, and I want to make it burn brightly as possible before handing it on to future generations.

GEORGE BERNARD SHAW, PLAYWRIGHT

AUGUST 27

I thought the fire
was out.
I stirred the ashes
I burnt my fingers.

ANTONIO MACHADO, POET

AUGUST 28

We all carry deep inside the part of us that hopes we can befriend life – that we can make a difference.

RACHEL NAOMI REMEN, PHYSICIAN AND WRITER

AUGUST 29

Life is not nearly so hard when we honor the self.

HYMEYOHST STORM, WRITER

AUGUST 30

*H*umanity has been sleeping – and still sleeps – lulled within the narrowly confining joys of its little closed loves. In the depths of the human multitude there slumbers an immense spiritual power which will manifest itself only when we have learnt how to break through the dividing walls of our egoism and raise ourselves up to an entirely new perspective, so that habitually and in a practical fashion we fix our gaze on universal realities.

TEILHARD DE CHARDIN, PALEONTOLOGIST

AUGUST 31

*A*nd you shall know yourselves that you are in God and God is in you. And you are the City of God.

NEW TESTAMENT APOCRYPHA

SEPTEMBER

Right Relationship

A bumper sticker proclaims:
Not he who dies with the most toys;
not he who cries with the most noise;
but he who tries with the most poise.

Trying "with the most poise" is about keeping a fine balance in our lives — being in right relationship. It is the care and values we embrace to create a good life for ourselves and for others. The freedoms of democracy are lived by being in right relationship — with people, laws, money, possessions, nature . . . and with our own spirit and purpose.

Above the din of money interests and rampant consumerism — a greater democracy shouts to us. It is time to be in right relationship with people and possession — to support ourselves and the good of all. It is time to vote for political leaders who earn our trust and admiration. And maybe it is time to become political leaders ourselves. Winston Churchill tells us, "we make a living by what we get, we make a life by what we give."

September 1

As my high school teacher, Miss Julia Coleman, used to say: "We must adjust to changing times and still hold to unchanging principles."

JIMMY CARTER, US PRESIDENT, 1977-1981

September 2

Principles only mean something when you stick to them when it is inconvenient.

THE CONTENDER, HOLLYWOOD FILM

September 3

Democracy is not so much a form of government as a set of principles.

WOODROW WILSON, US PRESIDENT, 1913-1921

SEPTEMBER 4

*T*o say that democracy is only a form of government is like saying home is a more or less geometrical arrangement of bricks and mortar; that the church is a building with pews, pulpit and spire. It is true they certainly are so much. But it is false, they are infinitely more. The real importance of democracy lay in its larger ethical meaning. Broadly conceived, democracy is a way of life, a form of moral and spiritual association, and a democratic form of government is but one of its manifestations.

JOHN DEWEY, EDUCATOR AND PHILOSOPHER

SEPTEMBER 5

*T*he measure of humankind is not in accumulated knowledge or possessions or proliferating pleasures and amusements. It must be in the nobility of personal intent – in the carefulness of the gesture each person makes.

SHERI RITCHLIN, SCHOLAR IN ASIAN PHILOSOPHY

SEPTEMBER 6

*W*ealth does not diminish by giving charity.

MUSLIM HADITH [SACRED TEACHING]

SEPTEMBER 7

*O*ur social and economic statistics are telling us what we already know in our hearts: we have created a world that works for only a few. To change this, we must learn to act toward each other and our environment in profoundly different ways.

VACLAV HAVEL, PRESIDENT, CZECH REPUBLIC, 1993-2003

SEPTEMBER 8

*T*he creative artist, poet, and saint must fight the actual (as opposed to the ideal) gods of our society – the god of conformism, as well as the gods of apathy, material success and exploitative power. These are the idols of society that are worshipped by multitudes of people.

ROLLO MAY, AUTHOR

SEPTEMBER 9

*O*ne great thing about democracies is that they make it very hard for secrets to be kept forever, for claims to go unchallenged indefinitely and for those in power to escape responsibility.

E.J. DIONNE, NEWSPAPER COLUMNIST

SEPTEMBER 10

*W*e meet and just keep talking until there's nothing left but the obvious truth.

OREN LYONS, TURTLE CLAN, ONONDAGA IROQUOIS.

SEPTEMBER 11

*G*overnment, on the old system, is an assumption of power, for the aggrandizement of itself; on the new, a delegation of power for the common benefit of society. The former supports itself by keeping up a system of war; the latter promotes a system of peace, as the true means of enriching a Nation.

THOMAS PAINE, STATESMAN

SEPTEMBER 12

*I*t is not power that corrupts, but fear. Fear of losing power corrupts those who wield it, and fear of the scourge of power corrupts those who are subject to it. Political interest can never be separated in the long run from moral right.

THOMAS JEFFERSON, US PRESIDENT, 1801-1809

SEPTEMBER 13

I am convinced that if we are to get on the right side of the world revolution, we as a nation must undergo a radical revolution of values. We must rapidly begin the shift from a `thing-oriented' society to a `person-oriented' society. When machines and computers, profit motives and property rights, are considered more important than people, the giant triplets of racism, materialism, and militarism are incapable of being conquered . . .

MARTIN LUTHER KING, JR., CIVIL RIGHTS LEADER

SEPTEMBER 14

*W*e have inherited the notion that democracy has to do only with the structure of government . . . it has been assumed that economic life lies largely outside democracy – a big mistake, because economics so determines our well being.

FRANCES MOORE LAPPÉ, FOUNDER, CENTER FOR LIVING DEMOCRACY

SEPTEMBER 15

*I*t is said that democracy is not something we have, but something we do. But right now we cannot do it because we cannot speak. We are shouted down by the bullhorns of big money. It is money with no manners for democracy, and it must be escorted from the room.

DORIS HADDOCK, POLITICAL ACTIVIST

SEPTEMBER 16

*W*e can have a democratic society or we can have great concentrated wealth in the hands of a few. We cannot have both.

LOUIS BRANDEIS, JUSTICE, US SUPREME COURT

SEPTEMBER 17

*W*e must all live so that our children do not have to pay for our deeds.

ANDREJS UPITS, LATVIAN AUTHOR

⁓

SEPTEMBER 18

*W*e are so busy protecting against that we have forgotten what we are living for.

SHERI RITCHLIN, SCHOLAR IN ASIAN PHILOSOPHY

⁓

SEPTEMBER 19

*H*alf of the confusion in the world comes from not knowing how little we need . . . I live more simply now, and with more peace.

RICHARD EVELYN BYRD, EXPLORER

SEPTEMBER 20

*W*hat was of ultimate concern in life ceased to be your relationship to the Divine and centered instead on your relationship to your income. And thus, even in the midst of economic plenty, your soul could slowly starve to death.

KEN WILBER, TRANSPERSONAL PHILOSOPHER

SEPTEMBER 21

*O*ften people attempt to live their lives backwards: they try to have more things or more money in order to do more of what they want so that they will be happier. The way it actually works is the reverse. You must first be who you really are, then do what you need to do in order to have what you want.

MARGARET YOUNG, AUTHOR

SEPTEMBER 22

I talk boldly like I do 'cause I know there is some kind of justice that we deserve.

TRICIA PEOPLES, COMMUNITY ORGANIZER

SEPTEMBER 23

We look forward to a world founded upon four essential
freedoms:
freedom of speech and expression . . . everywhere in the world
freedom of every person to worship God in his own way . . .
everywhere in the world
freedom from want . . . everywhere in the world.
freedom from fear . . . anywhere in the world.

FRANKLIN DELANO ROOSEVELT, US PRESIDENT, 1933-1945

SEPTEMBER 24

*A*ll the rights guaranteed by the Constitution were based on a vision of human nature that calls us to be responsible human beings – responsible to something within ourselves that is higher than the all too human desires for personal gain and satisfaction; higher than the dictates of the purely theoretical mind, higher than the instinctive loyalties to family and tribe.

JACOB NEEDLEMAN, PHILOSOPHER

SEPTEMBER 25

*W*ashing one's hands of the conflict between the powerful and the powerless means to side with the powerful, not to be neutral.

PAOLO FREIRE, EDUCATOR

SEPTEMBER 26

*W*e are not here merely to make a living. We are here to enrich the world, and we impoverish ourselves if we forget this errand.

WOODROW WILSON, US PRESIDENT, 1913-1921

SEPTEMBER 27

*O*ur task is not merely to boost the economy for a year or two. Our task is to prepare for a different and a better world. The times call for substantial departures and for a reaffirmation of what our country ought to stand for in the world.

JOHN K. GALBRAITH, ECONOMIST

SEPTEMBER 28

*E*very violation of truth is not only a sort of suicide in the liar, but is a stab at the health of human society.

RALPH WALDO EMERSON, WRITER AND POET

SEPTEMBER 29

I do still believe that there is within most of us a basic desire to live uprightly and kindly with our neighbors, but I also feel that we are at present in the grip of a wave of fear which threatens to overcome us. I think we need a rude awakening . . . to make us willing to sacrifice all that we have from the material standpoint in order that freedom and democracy may not perish from this earth.

ELEANOR ROOSEVELT, A CO-AUTHOR OF
UNIVERSAL DECLARATION OF HUMAN RIGHTS

SEPTEMBER 30

*W*hile I see transforming democracy as a challenge, it is by no means impossible to change. After all, it is a system formed by the people, for the people. For this reason, it is time for us to reclaim a governing process that has become dominated by corporate interests and the rich, and make it our own.

MEG ANSARA, YOUNG DEMOCRATIC VISIONARY

OCTOBER

Love in Action

Lovingkindness is essential for positive change in ourselves and our communities. When we participate in creating a greater democracy, our loving actions are also civic actions. And, our lovingkindness is not only for the "other person" but for our own soul's contentment as well.

The most honorable form of human love endures, commits, speaks up, tells the truth, and stops injustice. With lovingkindness as our core alignment, our lives are suffused with meaning.

The great spiritual teachers raise the power of love as humanity's highest destiny. What better means exists to help us create a greater democracy for our children and grandchildren? Ralph Waldo Emerson reminds us that the "power of love as the basis of a state has never been tried." Let's try it.

October 1

When I speak of love I am not speaking of some sentimental and weak response which is little more than emotional bosh. I am speaking of that force which all the great religions have seen as the supreme unifying principle of life. Love is somehow the key that unlocks the door that leads to ultimate reality.

MARTIN LUTHER KING, JR., CIVIL RIGHTS LEADER

October 2

As the Civil War progressed those who came in touch with Lincoln were more and more astonished by his absence of malice toward the Confederacy and its leaders. Slowly, deliberately, Lincoln directed the war toward victory with a patience and a will that became visible only over time, as in the words of one observer, "those who had sought cunningly to lead him, slowly found that he was leading them."

CARL SANDBURG, POET AND WRITER

October 3

There is comfort in the strength of love; t'will make a thing endurable, which else would overset the brain or break the heart.

WILLIAM WORDSWORTH, POET AND WRITER

October 4

If human beings can be trained for cruelty and greed and a belief in power which comes through hate and fear and force, certainly we can train equally well for gentleness and mercy and the power of love which comes because of the strength of the good qualities to be found in the soul of every individual human being.

ELEANOR ROOSEVELT, A CO-AUTHOR OF
UNIVERSAL DECLARATION OF HUMAN RIGHTS

October 5

My church is this chapel of democracy that we sit in together. Hate and anger have no place residing in the chapel of democracy . . .

THE CONTENDER, HOLLYWOOD FILM

OCTOBER 6

Lord, make me an instrument of Your peace.
Where there is hatred let me sow love;
Where there is injury, pardon;
Where there is doubt, faith;
Where there is despair hope;
Where there is darkness, light
Where there is sadness, joy.
O divine Master,
Grant that I may seek not so much to be consoled,
As to console;
Not so much to be understood,
As to understand;
Not so much to be loved,
As to love.
For it is in giving that we receive.
It is in pardoning that we are pardoned.
It is in dying that we awaken to eternal life.

ST. FRANCIS OF ASSISI

OCTOBER 7

*W*hat we need in the United States is not division. What we
need in the United States is not hatred. What we need in the
United States is not violence or lawlessness, but love and wisdom and

compassion toward one another, and a feeling of justice toward those who still suffer within our country whether they be white or they be black. Let us dedicate ourselves to what the Greeks wrote so many years ago: To tame the savageness of man and make gentle the life of this world. Let us dedicate ourselves to that and say a prayer for our country and our people.

ROBERT F. KENNEDY, US ATTORNEY GENERAL

OCTOBER 8

*T*he authority of the world order simply cannot be built on anything else but the revitalized authority of the universe. And how is this authority discovered? We need to draw upon the expanded ways of knowing beyond our narrow empiricism and rationalism – the wider epistemologies of the heart. We need to enter into that which we seek to know.

VACLAV HAVEL, PRESIDENT, CZECH REPUBLIC, 1933-2003

OCTOBER 9

*I*f our actions are truly to lessen suffering in the world, and not just shift it around a little, they have to come from the deepest quietest spaces of our hearts.

RAM DASS, SPIRITUAL TEACHER

OCTOBER 10

A man has a right to be employed, to be trusted, to be loved, to be revered. The power of love as the basis of state has never been tried.

RALPH WALDO EMERSON, POET AND WRITER

OCTOBER 11

I love America more than any other country in the world, and exactly for this reason, I insist on the right to criticize her perpetually.

JAMES BALDWIN, AUTHOR

OCTOBER 12

I n truth, at the rate the consciousness and the ambitions of the world are increasing, it will explode unless it learns to love. The future of the thinking earth is organically bound up with the turning of the forces of hate into forms of charity.

PIERRE TEILHARD DE CHARDIN, PALEONTOLOGIST

OCTOBER 13

*C*ompassion, kindness and concern can be found everywhere in America. And, if we have learned nothing else from this [Sept.11] tragedy, we have learned that our time on earth is short, so there is simply no time for hate.

SANDRA DAHL, WIFE OF JASON DAHL, PILOT, UNITED FLIGHT 93

OCTOBER 14

*W*e can't avoid using power so let us love powerfully.

MARTIN BUBER, THEOLOGIAN

OCTOBER 15

*T*he everyday kindness of the back roads more than makes up for the greed in the headlines.

CHARLES KURALT, JOURNALIST

OCTOBER 16

*I*n this generation, the fate of our natural environment and of our democratic environment will be decided. Only great leadership and great love can get us through the times ahead. We must all take part in this great drama. It is more than politics, it is a struggle for the soul, and it is exquisitely personal to each of us.

DORIS HADDOCK, POLITICAL ACTIVIST

OCTOBER 17

*N*othing worth doing is completed in our lifetime; therefore we must be saved by hope. Nothing true or beautiful makes complete sense in any immediate context of history; therefore we must be saved by faith. Nothing we do, however virtuous, can be accomplished alone; therefore, we are saved by love. Man's capacity for justice makes democracy possible, but man's inclination to injustice makes democracy necessary.

REINHOLD NIEBUHR, THEOLOGIAN

OCTOBER 18

Luke's Place

Nobody who knew Luke McArthur, a Catholic priest for 42 years, ever doubted what his life purpose was: to be a prophet who challenged civil and religious authority to open doors to poor or alienated people. Luke's purpose was clear and simple to everyone he connected with. And everyone who remembers Luke was influenced by his life.

In 1989, Luke retired as a pastor of a Milwaukee congregation, and he joined Community Advocates, a low-income organization, to develop a household goods warehouse for homeless families.

Project Second Start was more than a warehouse that collected and distributed furniture. It was Luke's Place where families who had lost everything in their homelessness, regained hope as they made a new start in life.

In developing Project Second Start, Luke parlayed his connections with people and organizations into a purpose-driven enterprise which today has thousands of Milwaukeeans contributing household goods, and thousands of homeless families able to make a second start in life.

Luke passed away in May of 1999. Today his spirit and purpose continues to live and thrive at Luke's Place. Luke made a difference when he moved among us. Even now, he is making a difference.

RAMON WAGNER, COMMUNITY ORGANIZER

OCTOBER 19

*L*aw is not just something that somebody wrote in Washington 200 years ago, in Mecca 1400 years ago, or in the desert of Sinai thousands of years before. It's something that is alive now. It's something that humans create out of love and justice. It can, by demonstrating compassion, affirm our unity and connectedness.

JONATHAN GRANOFF, PRESIDENT GLOBAL SECURITY INSTITUTE

OCTOBER 20

*I*n the midst of global crises such as pollution, wars and famine, kindness may too easily be dismissed as a "soft issue. . . . " But kindness is the greatest need in all those areas. . . . Until we reflect basic kindness in everything we do, our political gestures will be fleeting and fragile.

BO LOZOFF, CO-FOUNDER HUMAN KINDNESS FOUNDATION

OCTOBER 21

*C*aring is the greatest thing. Caring matters most.

FREIDRICH VON HUGEL, THEOLOGIAN (LAST WORDS BEFORE HE DIED)

October 22

There is no power greater than a community discovering what it cares about. Ask, "what's possible? Not, "what's wrong." Keep asking.

MARGARET WHEATLEY, CORPORATE CONSULTANT

October 23

Make a home.
Help make a community,
Be loyal to what you have made.

Put the interest of the community first.
Love your neighbors, not the neighbors you pick out, but the
    ones that you have.

Love this miraculous world that we did not make, that is a gift
    to us.
Find work, if you can, that does no damage.
Enjoy your work.
Work well.

WENDELL BERRY, POET AND WRITER

OCTOBER 24

*L*ike the grasses showing tender faces to each other, thus should we do, for this was the wish of the Grandfathers of the world.

BLACK ELK, HOLY MAN OGLALA SIOUX

OCTOBER 25

*L*ove is the energy that attaches you to life.

SHERI RITCHLIN, SCHOLAR IN ASIAN PHILOSOPHY

OCTOBER 26

*W*hat happens in your innermost being is worthy of your whole love.

RAINIER MARIA RILKE, POET AND WRITER

October 27

*H*e who loves brings God and the world together.

MARTIN BUBER, THEOLOGIAN

October 28

*H*uman beings cut off from a sense of usefulness and love can wither away and die. This is why depression is dangerous – it is disconnection from the vital energy. And it is why joy and happiness, a sense of usefulness and significance can be so potent in healing.

SHERI RITCHLIN, SCHOLAR IN ASIAN PHILOSOPHY

October 29

A new commandment I give to you, that you love one another even as I have loved you, that you also love one another.

JESUS OF NAZARETH
JOHN 13:34, RSV

OCTOBER 30

*L*et us transform the love of power into the power of love.

NIRMALA DESHPANDE, GANDHIAN EDUCATOR

OCTOBER 31

*S*omeday after we have mastered the winds, the waves, the tides and gravity, we shall harness for God, the energies of love. Then for the second time in history of the world, man will have discovered fire.

PIERRE TEILHARD DE CHARDIN, PALEONTOLOGIST

NOVEMBER

Cooperation

Cooperation means working together for a common purpose. If we cooperate with one another and with nature the planet will flourish. If we don't cooperate we won't make it. Cooperation is linked with service and directs us to see a need, reach out, and work with others to meet that need.

Cooperation is a life force for democracy because it means people working together to resolve difficulties. A thriving democracy does not remove problems from life, but says, "lend a hand, work together and the worst situations can be improved." Cooperation and service are no longer just nice words but are planetary survival skills. Ordinary people cooperating with one another are the real tour-de-force fueling a greater democracy.

November 1

The most creative turn of events in man's long history occurred when man set down his stone ax and began to cooperate with his neighbor. That seemingly elementary decision set in motion what we now know as civilization.

MARTIN LUTHER KING, JR., CIVIL RIGHTS LEADER

November 2

A new idea has been born to the children of industry. Co-operation has dawned upon the world. Co-operation is the next big step. . . . This [co-operation] is the true remedy for the ills of society. . . . This is the great idea that is destined to break down the present system of centralization, monopoly and extortion.

WILLIAM H. SYLVUS, LABOR LEADER, 1864

NOVEMBER 3

*C*ooperation is not a bargaining game in which one person's success is achieved at the expense or exclusion of the success of others. The constant aim of cooperation is mutual benefit in human interactions; it is governed by the principle of mutual respect. . . .

JAYANTI KIRPALINI AND MOHINI PANJABI, SPIRITUAL TEACHERS

NOVEMBER 4

*S*ervice was as much a part of my upbringing as eating breakfast and going to school. It isn't something that you do in your spare time. It was clear that it was the very purpose of life. In that context you are not obligated to win. You are obligated to keep trying, to keep doing the best you can everyday.

MARIAN WRIGHT EDELMAN, FOUNDER, CHILDREN'S DEFENSE FUND

NOVEMBER 5

*A*sk yourself at the end of each day, what did I learn? who did I help?

ZINA JACQUES, EDUCATOR

NOVEMBER 6

*J*t is high time that the ideal of success should be replaced by the ideal of service.

ALBERT EINSTEIN, PHYSICIST

NOVEMBER 7

Presidential Inaugural Address, 1960:

. . . And if a beachhead of cooperation may push back the jungle of suspicion, let both sides join in creating a new endeavor, not a new balance of power, but a new world of law, where the strong are just and the weak secure and the peace preserved.

All this will not be finished in the first one hundred days. Nor will it be finished in the first one thousand days, nor in the life of this Administration, nor even perhaps in our lifetime on this planet. But let us begin. In your hands, my fellow citizens, more than mine, will rest the final success or failure of our course.

JOHN F. KENNEDY, US PRESIDENT, 1961-1963

NOVEMBER 8

In our world of big names, curiously, our true heroes tend to be anonymous . . . the teacher, the nurse, the mother, the honest cop, the hard workers at lonely underpaid, unglamorous, unpublicized jobs.

DANIEL J. BOORSTIN, HISTORIAN

NOVEMBER 9

When we are cooperating we act in accord with the natural laws which have kept the species unfolding and growing and learning for this last two million years . . . the true story of humanity is that being friends and having neighbors is what works; it is what makes us more secure. We know that.

CRAIG BARNES, POLITICAL COMMENTATOR

NOVEMBER 10

It is our special duty, that if anyone needs our help, we should give him such help to the utmost of our power.

CICERO, STATESMAN AND WRITER

November 11

*N*o person among us desires any other reward for performing a brave and worthy action, but the consciousness of having served his nation.

JOSEPH BRANT, MOHAWK LEADER

November 12

Look up and not down.
Look forward and not back.
Look out and not in.
Lend a hand.

EDWARD EVERETT HALE, CLERGYMAN

November 13

*N*ever miss a good chance to shut up.

WILL ROGERS, HUMORIST

*R*ather than fighting we're negotiating . . . rather than suing each other, we're putting together teams and combining resources to properly manage the natural resources we all depend on . . . it takes a lot of patience, but there's more good people than bad people and the system will work if we all get in there and take part and stay committed. That's the only way we can get our salmon back and our waters clean.

BILLY FRANK, COMMUNITY ORGANIZER

I must say that I have seen Americans make great and real sacrifices to the public welfare; and I have noticed a hundred instances in which they hardly ever failed to lend faithful support to one another.

ALEXIS DE TOCQUEVILLE, HISTORIAN

NOVEMBER 16

*A*cting in concert, we do make a difference in the quality of our lives, our institutions, our environment and our planetary future. Through cooperation, we manifest the essential spirit that unites us amidst our diverse ways.

AVON MATTISON, PEACE ACTIVIST

NOVEMBER 17

*T*he conditions which surround us best justify our cooperation: we meet in the midst of a nation brought to the verge of moral, political and material ruin. Corruption dominates the ballot box, the legislatures, the Congress, and even touches the ermine of the bench. . . .

THE POPULIST PLATFORM, 1892

*T*he world is moved along, not only by the mighty shoves of its heroes, but also by the aggregate of the tiny pushes of each honest worker.

HELEN KELLER, HUMANITARIAN

*B*ut if there was one thing President Kennedy stood for that touched the most profound feelings of people around the world, it was the belief that idealism . . . and deep convictions are not incompatible with the most practical and efficient of programs – that there is no basic inconsistency between ideals and realistic possibilities, no separation between the deepest desires of heart and mind and the rational application of human effort to human problems.

ROBERT F. KENNEDY, US ATTORNEY GENERAL

November 20

*P*eople see God everyday, they just don't recognize him.

PEARL BAILEY, SINGER

November 21

*H*elp your brother's boat across and your own has reached the shore.

HINDU PROVERB

November 22

*T*he most solid comfort one can fall back upon is the thought that the business of one's life is to help in some small way to reduce the sum of ignorance, degradation and misery on the face of the earth.

GEORGE ELIOT, AUTHOR

NOVEMBER 23

*D*o what you think is right to help other people without expecting recognition.

TONY REYNA, GOVERNOR, TAOS PUEBLO

~~

NOVEMBER 24

*F*ear less, hope more; eat less, chew more; whine less, breathe more; hate less, love more, and all good things are yours.

SWEDISH PROVERB

Compassion Cells

As a response to terror and the focus on "terrorist cells," we started a citizens group in Orange County California called "compassion cells" that focus on compassionate actions. "Compassion cells" are exactly opposite of terrorist cells – we organize projects to improve social conditions locally and globally. We work for change by working together. One "compassion cell" recently fed 200 people at a downtown armory. We are planning interfaith seminars in local prisons and homeless shelters.

A "compassion cell" can be anywhere and consist of a few people engaging in one selfless act or an entire community. They function on the principle of kindness. The idea is potentially contagious and totters on pandemic proportions as people self-organize compassion cells everywhere in the world.

JASON THOMAS, FOUNDER, COMPASSION CELLS

NOVEMBER 26

I don't know how much it costs when America or any other country builds a chemical or nuclear weapon to throw a heavy bomb at any country in the world. But I know that there are many, many children, who die because they can't buy food and they don't have the necessary medical care. Is that the justice you talk about? You use maybe one billion dollars to throw away a bomb and let many children die from the hunger and then you call your self a liberator. Why don't we help each other? We all are human.

MOHAMED, A TEENAGED BOY CURRENTLY LIVING IN PALESTINE

∽

NOVEMBER 27

*T*he motivating force for the theory of a democratic way of life is still a belief that as individuals we live co-operatively and, to the best of our ability, serve the community in which we live, and that our own success, to be real, must contribute to the success of others.

ELEANOR ROOSEVELT,
AUTHOR OF UNIVERSAL DECLARATION OF HUMAN RIGHTS

∽

NOVEMBER 28

*U*nless individuals can stretch the limits of what they believe possible, and unless we can learn how to work together in a collective effort, even the best technology can't help us.

DOUGLAS ENGELBART, INTERNET NETWORK ENGINEER

*F*or though we may renounce the world for ourselves, refuse the attempt to get anything out of it, we have to accept it as the sphere in which we are to co-operate with the Spirit, and try to do the Will. Therefore the prevalent notion that spirituality and politics have nothing to do with one another is the exact opposite of the truth.

EVELYN UNDERHILL, SPIRITUAL TEACHER

NOVEMBER 30

May the seasons
Bear their gifts upon you.
May your heart be soothed
By the warmth of others,
May your prayers
Be taken into the heavens
And answered in their time.
May your journey
Be traveled with rejoicing.
Your existence
A blessing to another
Along the way.

HOWARD RAINER, POET

DECEMBER

Agents of Change

What does it take to be an effective agent of change? Some agents of change describe themselves as pragmatic visionaries. They see things as they are, imagine things as they could be and get to work. It takes head and heart, commitment and compassion to make a difference in the world. Marilyn King, a former US Olympian, trains young adults in the skills needed for peacemaking. She knows that winning athletes, citizens, and peacemakers are alike — they must all exert effort — skill, muscle, sweat and tears to reach their goals. Standing against the status quo, following a vision, falling down and getting up, trusting that you can do it — are skills required of athletes and citizens alike. A greater democracy will not evolve without people like us, who say, "yes, I am a "citizen athlete" one of many agents of positive change. Even now as I think of what's possible for me to do, I am becoming the change I want to see."

DECEMBER 1

*D*emocracy is based on the conviction that there are extraordinary possibilities in ordinary people.

HARRY EMERSON FOSDICK, CLERGYMAN

DECEMBER 2

*D*emocracy is never a thing done. Democracy is always something a nation must be doing. What is necessary now is one thing and one thing only, that democracy become again democracy in action, not democracy accomplished and piled up in goods and gold.

ARCHIBALD MACLEISH, POET

DECEMBER 3

*I*t is not because things are difficult that we do not dare. It is because we do not dare that things are difficult.

SENECA, STATESMAN

DECEMBER 4

Daring to Dream a Compassionate Political System

I want my government leaders to be thoughtful human beings who listen deeply and lead with compassion. I believe that one thing blocking this kind of leadership is my own ability to see that political leaders are no different from me but are people just like me who need support and who struggle to balance the spiritual and political dimensions of life.

Inspired by the teachings of Zen Buddhist master, Thich Nhat Hanh, we created the Committee on Mindful Politics. Our mission is to support just, compassionate, and courageous leadership and to deepen mutual understanding between policy makers and constituents. Our first action came directly after September 11, 2001 when we launched the "love letter" campaign. We called on people to write a letter to their representative to ask them to do nothing. We asked them to breathe. This radical notion was met with appreciation not resistance.

Two years later, we held a retreat for Congress led by Thich Nhat Hanh. Eleven members of Congress and their spouses engaged in silent meditation practices and listened to teachings about how to maintain spiritual balance in a hectic life. Thich Nhat Hanh's words were simple and no different than anything he would tell any other practitioner. The impact was profound. The ripples may never be measured but when 11 members of Congress give up two days to engage in compassionate listening and silent contemplation, I believe the government that I dare to dream is possible.

CAROLYN CLEVELAND, CITIZEN

DECEMBER 5

*A*s we build wise democracies, all the good things people are trying to do for the world will become so much easier to accomplish.

TOM ATLEE, FOUNDER, CO-INTELLIGENCE INSTITUTE

DECEMBER 6

*A*n informed and connected citizenship provides the best leadership on Earth.

JIM FOURNIER, INTERNET NETWORK ENGINEER

DECEMBER 7

Mardy Murie

*N*ews of her death spread across the county, moving many people to pause and reflect on the inspirational life of Mardy Murie. Mardy and her husband Olaus devoted their lives advocating for wild places. Their advocacy grew from a deep love and intimate relationship with wilderness. Together, the Muries worked on legislation that eventually became the Wilderness Act that was signed into law in 1964. At age 78 Mardy worked with President Jimmy Carter to create the Alaska Lands Act which put aside millions of acres for national parks and wildlife refuges. Friends said that Mardy could see the magical in the mundane and always had a quote on her mantle.

John Turner, a native of Moose, Wyoming, and now working in Washington DC said, "both Mardy and Olaus were folks who exemplified gentle spirits yet strong wills and strong commitments. Mardy had gentle respect for people even though she disagreed, and yet could state a very strong case. . . . Mardy was a reminder to all of us that we need to embrace a spirit that is integral to the American experience, and that's wilderness."

WHITNEY ROYSTER, NEWS REPORTER

DECEMBER 8

*T*he best defense against usurpatory government is an assertive citizenry.

WILLIAM F. BUCKLEY, POLITICAL COMMENTATOR

Gettysburg Address

*F*our score and seven years ago our fathers brought forth, upon this continent, a new nation, conceived in Liberty, and dedicated to the proposition that all men are created equal.

Now we are engaged in a great civil war, testing whether that nation, or any nation, so conceived, and so dedicated, can long endure. We are met here on a great battlefield of that war. We have come to dedicate a portion of it as a final resting place for those who here gave their lives that that nation might live. It is altogether fitting and proper that we should do this.

But in a larger sense we can not dedicate – we can not consecrate – we can not hallow this ground. The brave men, living and dead, who struggled, here, have consecrated it far above our poor power to add or detract. The world will little note, nor long remember, what we say here, but can never forget what they did here. It is for us, the living, rather to be dedicated here to the unfinished work which they have, thus far, so nobly carried on. It is rather for us to be here dedicated to the great task remaining before us – that from these honored dead we take increased devotion to that cause for which they here gave the last full measure of devotion – that we here highly resolve that these dead shall not have died in vain; that this nation shall have a new birth of freedom; and that this government of the people, by the people, for the people, shall not perish from the earth.

ABRAHAM LINCOLN, US PRESIDENT, 1861-1865

DECEMBER 10

[After hearing the Gettysburg Address] the crowd departed with a new thing in its ideological luggage, that new Constitution Lincoln had substituted for the one they brought there with them. They walked off, from those curving graves on the hillside, under a changed sky, into a different America. Lincoln had revolutionized the revolution, giving people a new past to live with that would change their future indefinitely.

GARRY WILLS, AUTHOR

DECEMBER 11

The hundreds of thousands of our dead, buried in rows upon rows in our national cemeteries, sacrificed their lives for a democracy of a free people, not for what we have today. It is up to each of us that these boys and girls did not die in vain. That's how serious this message is.

DORIS HADDOCK, POLITICAL ACTIVIST

DECEMBER 13

Compassionate Activism

I watched with foreboding our government's post 9.11 growing military stance and I reflected on the teachings of Thich Nhat Hanh, a role model of mine. I tried to apply his teachings to help me understand my emotions and help others with theirs. Later, as war broke, I attended protests at school and saw both sides angrily yelling insults at the other. At one event, my friend and I left the hostile protesters, walked away quietly, and he burst into tears. It seemed all we knew how to do was to muster power through verbal violence.

I became more involved in protesting the war – but I decided to sit in silent meditation on campus with a large sign next to me. One message on the sign said:

> If you are interested in my reasons [for protesting against the war], please consider asking me, and I promise to do my best to speak respectfully and respond to counter-arguments thoughtfully and with fact and feeling. I hope we can discuss the issue, even if you have a position you believe at this point to be different than my own. Peace.

All in all, 400 people stopped in front of me and about 50 engaged me in conversation. By the last week, I felt I was making a difference. My "protest action" inspired my friends and peers to start a dialogue group about campus activism. We are talking about how to use compassionate action as a practical means for effective protest and community work.

MICHAEL D. FLISS, COMPASSIONATE ACTIVIST

December 14

We are at that very point in time when a 400-year-old age is dying and another is struggling to be born – a shifting of culture, science, society, and institutions enormously greater than the world has ever experienced. Ahead, the possibility of the regeneration of individuality, liberty, community, and ethics such as the world has never known, and a harmony with nature, with one another, and with the divine intelligence such as the world has never dreamed.

DEE HOCK, FOUNDER VISA INTERNATIONAL

December 15

A march for disarmament reforms, organized by Viva Rio a large NGO [non-governmental organization] in Rio de Janeiro, was a great success. Even though it was cold and raining more than 50,000 people showed up and demanded the Parliament approve the disarmament law. That evening, a famous soap opera included images and scenes of the march. That way, over 60 million Brazilians learned about the importance of passing this law. It is hard to describe the positive feeling of actually doing an event like this with your own hands. I kept praying that activities like this would be reproduced everywhere.

On October 24, 2003, The Disarmament Statute passed the Congress of Brazil and sweeping gun reforms became law.

It is a ten year saga with a happy ending. Now the focus is on enforcement. We hope that our example can be a source of inspiration for all peoples and nations. We are ready to help. If we are able to envision a gun free planet it is the first step for transforming this wild world.

ANDRÉ PORTO, SPIRITUAL ACTIVIST

D E C E M B E R   1 6

*T*he challenge of adulthood is holding onto your idealism after you have lost your innocence.

BRUCE SPRINGSTEEN, SINGER AND SONGWRITER

D E C E M B E R   1 7

*S*hoot for the moon – even if you miss you will land among the stars.

LES BROWN, PROFESSIONAL SPEAKER

DECEMBER 18

We're here for a reason. I believe a bit of the reason is to throw little torches out to lead people through the dark.

WHOOPI GOLDBERG, ACTRESS

DECEMBER 19

"The people," said a farmer's wife in a Minnesota country store while her husband was buying a new pot hole digger, "The people," she went on, "will stick around and last a long time. The people run the works, only they don't know it yet – you wait and see."

CARL SANDBURG, POET AND WRITER

DECEMBER 20

*T*he eight-hour day, the minimum wage, the conservation of natural resources and the protection of our air, water, and land, women's rights and civil rights, free trade unions, Social Security and a civil service based on merit all these were launched as citizen's movements and won the endorsement of the political class only after long struggles and in the face of bitter opposition and sneering attacks. It's just a fact: Democracy doesn't work without citizen activism and participation, starting at the community.

BILL MOYERS, JOURNALIST

DECEMBER 21

*N*o shift in the way we think or act is more critical than this: we must put people at the center of everything we do. That is the essence of human security.

KOFI ANNAN, SECRETARY-GENERAL UNITED NATIONS

December 22

The new democracy depends upon you and me. It depends upon you and me because there is no one else in the world but you and me. If I pledge myself to the new democracy and you pledge yourself to the new democracy, a new moral force will be born in the world.

MARY PARKER FOLLETT, VISIONARY

December 23

Here in America we are descended in blood and in spirit from revolutionaries and rebels – men and women who dared to dissent from accepted doctrine. As their heirs, may we never confuse honest dissent with disloyal subversion.

DWIGHT D. EISENHOWER, US PRESIDENT, 1953-1961

DECEMBER 24

*O*ur choice is not whether change will come, but whether we can guide that change in the service of our ideals and toward a social order shaped to the needs of all our people. In the long run we can master change not through force or fear, but only through the free work of an understanding mind, through an openness to knowledge and fresh outlooks which can only strengthen the most fragile and the most powerful of human gifts: the gift of reason.

ROBERT F. KENNEDY, US ATTORNEY GENERAL

DECEMBER 25

*W*hen people decide they want to be free . . . there is nothing that can stop them.

DESMOND TUTU, ANGLICAN BISHOP

December 26

*Y*ou remember those two! I once mentioned them to you. You said, "they're harmless dreamers and they're loved by the people." "What," I asked is harmless about the love of the people?" Revolution only needs good dreamers who remember their dreams and the love of the people.

TENNESSEE WILLIAMS, PLAYWRIGHT

December 27

*W*e can improve America for all its citizens and future generations if we work hard and have hope. We are living examples of Gandhi's credo that you have to be the change you want to see in the world. There is a clear and present danger and the clock is rapidly ticking away. . . . Failure is not an option. . . . If not now, when? If not us, who?

STEPHANIE SANCHEZ, DAVE LEAHY, YAEL MUHLRAD,
YOUNG DEMOCRATIC VISIONARIES

DECEMBER 28

I am a journalist. I did not gather the facts and arrange them patiently for permanent preservation and laboratory analysis. My purpose was . . . to see if the shameful facts, spread out in all their shame, would not burn through our civic shamelessness and set fire to American pride.

LINCOLN STEFFENS, JOURNALIST, POPULIST PARTY

DECEMBER 29

We dare not forget today that we are the heirs of that first revolution. Let the word go forth from this time and place, to friend and foe alike, that the torch has been passed to a new generation of Americans – born in this century, tempered by war, disciplined by a hard and bitter peace, proud of our ancient heritage – and unwilling to witness or permit the slow undoing of those human rights to which this nation has always been committed, and to which we are committed today at home and around the world.

JOHN FITZGERALD KENNEDY, US PRESIDENT, 1961-1963

DECEMBER 30

*I*n this possible terminal phase of human existence, democracy and freedom are more than just ideas to be valued – they may be essential for survival.

NOAM CHOMKSY, LINGUIST

DECEMBER 31

*H*ow we measure up will depend in large part on today's leaders, especially those who chart the course of the world's one remaining superpower. But, what will be decisive is whether or not in sufficient numbers men and women in "small places close to home" can imagine and then begin to live the reality of freedom, solidarity, and peace.

MARY ANN GLENDON, HISTORIAN

Index of Sources Quoted

Ansara, Meg – Contributor to 2020 Vision, Ansara was the Massachusetts organizer for Stand for the Children, a national organization that brings local communities together to find lasting solutions to issues facing children. *www.2020Democrats.org.* p. 139

Anthony, Susan B. – A legendary American abolitionist, educational reformer, labor activist, temperance worker, suffragist, and women's rights campaigner. p. 36

Aristotle – A 4th-century Greek philosopher who, unlike his teacher Plato, saw ultimate reality not in ideas but in physical objects knowable through experience. His philosophical and scientific systems have been a major force in Western intellectual history. p. 26

Assembly of 5000 People, Kazakhstan. p. 68

Atlee, Tom – Founder of Co-Intelligence Institute, Atlee writes on politics and democratic transformation and provides information about democracy to thousands of people via the Internet. Atlee's most recent book is *The Tao of Democracy.* *www.co-intelligence org.* pp. 50, 58, 61, 100, 108, 172

Aung Sung Suu Kyi –1991 Nobel Peace Laureate and world-renowned advocate for democratic freedom and dignity in Burma, Aung Sung Suu Kyi has undergone house detention and imprisonment because of her struggle. Her recent books include *Letters from Burma*, 1998, *Freedom from Fear and Other Writings*, 1996, and, *The Voice of Hope*, 1997. pp. 31, 120

B

Bachelard, Gaston – French philosopher Bachelard considered imagination and reverie as well as reason to be creative forces in knowing. His *On Poetic Imagination and Reverie* was published in 1971. p. 49

Bailey, Pearl – A consummate entertainer with a strong personal commitment to helping others. Pearl Bailey served as the US goodwill ambassador to the United

Nations and received the Living Legacy Award in 1989, which honors humanitarian service. p. 164

Bahro, Rudoph – An economist known by some to be a Marxist, Bahro writes about political ecology. His books include *The Alternative in Eastern Europe*, 1981. p. 96

Baldwin, James – Major American novelist, playwright, and essayist. Baldwin's best-known works include *Go Tell It On the Mountain*, 1953, *Notes of a Native Son*, 1955, and *The Fire Next Time*, 1963. p. 140

Barnes, Craig – International lawyer and political commentator, Barnes received a standing ovation for his talk "History is On Our Side," sponsored by the Veterans for Peace, in Santa Fe, New Mexico, 2003. pp. 52, 59, 159

Bernstein, Leonard – American conductor and composer Bernstein became music director of the New York Philharmonic in 1953. His successes include *West Side Story*, and many of his writings are published in *The Joy of Music*, 1959. His legacy endures in the Leonard Bernstein Center, a school that provides teachers with a model education program called Artful Learning. p. 105

Berry, Thomas – A Passionist priest and eco-theologian, Berry was among the first to say, "the earth crisis is fundamentally a spiritual crisis." Berry's books include, *Dream of the Earth*, 1988, and *The Great Work*, 1999. pp. 95, 97, 111

Berry, Wendell – Widely published writer of essays, poetry, fiction and biographies. Berry's voice is that of a farmer, husband, lover and environmentalist with a deep commitment to regional sensibilities and nature's gifts. pp. 75, 151

Black Elk – A renowned Oglala Sioux holy man. In 1930, Black Elk recounted his stories and visions to John G. Neihardt, in a work entitled *Black Elk Speaks, Being the Life Story of a Holy Man of the Oglala Sioux*. pp. 25, 152

Black National Anthem – Official song of the NAACP. Words by poet James Weldon Johnson and music by J. Rosamond Johnson, 1921. p. 44

Block, Peter – Consultant and speaker Block focuses on bringing service and accountability to organizations. His books include *The Answer to How is Yes, Acting on What Matters, Stewardship, Choosing Service over Self-Interest*, and *The Empowered Manager, Positive Political Skills at Work*. p. 103

Boff, Leonardo – Theologian and an active member of the Christian community in Brazil. With the lifting of the Vatican ban on his publications, new writings by Boff are anticipated. His earlier writings include *Jesus Christ Liberator*,1978; *Liberating Grace*, 1979; and *Way of Cross Way of Justice*, 1980. p. 59

Boissiere, Robert – Author of several books on Hopi religion and culture, Boissiere is acclaimed as a Santa Fe living treasure, and his story is found in the book *Living Treasures of Santa Fe*, 1995. p. 92

Boorstin, Daniel J. – A renowned historian, Boorstin has written numerous books including *The Genius of American Politics, Democracy and Its Discontents*, and *The Lost World of Thomas Jefferson*. p. 159

Brandeis, Louis – Often called "the people's attorney," Brandeis was the first Jewish associate justice to serve on the Supreme Court, from 1916-1939. He fought industrial and financial monopoly and, after 1933, voted to uphold most of Franklin Roosevelt's New Deal legislation. p. 133

Brant, Joseph – A Mohawk Indian Chief known as Thayendanegea, Brant, fearing that the Indians would lose their lands if the colonists won, sided with the British during the American War of Independence. p. 160

Braun, Carol Moseley – Former US Senator from Illinois, Braun made news in 1992 when she was elected the first black woman to the Senate and again in 2003, when she became the second black woman to run for president. p. 62

Brooke, Gita – Gita and Anthony Brooke founded Peace Through Unity in 1975 because they were convinced that "the future lies in the hands of people of the world." Their story can be found in *Living Treasures of Santa Fe*, 1995. p. 120

Brown, Les – A professional speaker, author and television personality, Brown works to inspire people to live up to their greatness. p. 178

Buber, Martin – A leading 20th-century Jewish philosopher and theologian, Buber is renowned for his book *I and Thou*, 1923, which has had a profound effect on both Jewish and Christian theology. pp. 147, 153

Buck, Pearl S. – An American writer, Buck won the Pulitzer Prize in 1935 for her novel *The Good Earth*, set in China, where she lived for years; and in1938 she won the Nobel Prize for Literature. p. 93

Buckley, William F. – Columnist, TV commentator, and editor, Buckley founded the conservative journal *National Review* in 1955; and his *Firing Line* is the longest-running TV program in the US featuring the same host. p. 173

Burns, Ken – Founder of Florentine Films in 1976, Burns has produced several award winning videos, including *Civil War, Jazz, Thomas Jefferson,* and *Listening to Children. p.* 101

Byrd, Richard Evelyn – American explorer and Rear Admiral in the US Navy. From his base, Little America, in the Antarctic, Byrd conducted five major expeditions between 1930 and 1956. p. 134

C

Campbell, Joseph – Renowned mythologist Campbell is well-known for his influential book *Hero with a Thousand Faces*, 1949, and many other works, including *Myths to Live By*, 1972, and *The Mythic Image*, 1974. p. 89

Carlin, George – Comedian and author Carlin has won two Grammy Awards and is known for salty monologues and emphasis on social commentary. p. 95

Carse, James P. – Author and professor Carse taught history and literature at New York University. His writings explore how Judeo-Christian tradition has profound influence on the intellect and the imagination and include *Gospel of the Beloved Disciple*, 1997. p. 82

Carter, Jimmy – 39th US president (1977-1981), Carter was instrumental in producing the Camp David Accords, the peace treaty between Egypt and Israel, and is an advocate for human rights worldwide. The Carter Center, which he founded, addresses national and international issues of public policy. Carter received the 2002 Nobel Prize for Peace. p. 128

Castaneda, Carlos – Anthropologist and spiritual writer Castaneda deals with the teachings of his shaman and mentor, Don Juan – including the secrets of existence, dreaming, reality, and deciphering illusion. *Journey to Ixtlan, The Lesson of Don Juan*, 1978, is one of Castaneda's most popular books. p. 74

Cather, Willa – One of the most important American novelists of the early 20th century. Among her highly esteemed works are *My Antonia, O Pioneers, The Song of the Lark*, and *Death Comes for the Archbishop*, widely regarded as her masterpiece. p. 14.

Cato – The story and spirit of Cato, a field slave before the Civil War, are included in junior high school social studies curricula in the US. p. 45

Cervantes, Miguel de – The great Spanish dramatist, novelist, and poet Cervantes created one of world literature's most memorable figures in *Don Quixote de la Mancha* – a work that had a decisive impact on the development of the European novel. p. 105

Chapman, John Jay – Essayist and social commentator Chapman attacked the get-rich-quick mentality of the Gilded Age. Chapman's book *New Horizons in American Life*, 1932, attacked the way US education was dominated by the needs of business. p. 38

Chariots of Fire – 1981 award-winning film of two British subjects – both runners – after World War I, and their tireless pursuit of winning. It is a rich commentary on both the former British class society and the drive of the human spirit. p. 41

Chicago, Judy – Artist, author and feminist. Chicago's famed art work is *The Dinner Party*. Her books include *Through the Flower, My Struggles as a Woman Artist;* and *The Dinner Party: A Symbol of Our Heritage.* p. 55

Chisholm, Shirley – First black woman elected to Congress. In 1972, Chisholm also became the first black woman to run as a Democratic candidate for president. Her biography is *Unbought and Unbossed.* p. 33

Chittister, Sister Joan – A Benedictine nun, Sister Joan is an international lecturer and leading voice in spirituality. Currently, she is Executive Director of BenetVision: A Resource and Research Center for Contemporary Spirituality in Erie, PA. p. 114

Chomsky, Noam – Among the many provocative books by Chomsky, a leading American linguist and political analyst, are *Hegemony or Survival: America's Quest for Global Dominance*, 2003, and *Powers and Prospects, Reflections on Human Nature and the Social Order*, 1996. p. 185

Cicero – Roman orator, philosopher, senator, and statesman, whose life (196-43 BCE) coincided with the fall of the Roman Republic. Cicero's gifts made him one of Rome's most articulate citizens, and through him, Greek philosophy moved into Western Europe. p. 159

Citizens, Bloomington, Indiana. p. 80

Clark, Septima Pointsette – A teacher in South Carolina, Clark also worked with the Highlander Folk School in Tennessee. She established innovative citizenship schools and influenced thousands of people to stand up for their rights. p. 34

Cleveland, Carolyn – Founder of Committee for Mindful Politics in Washington, DC. p. 171

Cleveland, Harlan – A political scientist, public executive, and former assistant secretary of state, Cleveland is president emeritus of the World Academy of Arts and Sciences and has written many books on executive leadership and international affairs. pp. 51, 84

Cohen, Carl – A professor of philosophy at the University of Michigan, Cohen is author of several books, including *Affirmative Action and Racial Preference*, 2003; and *Democracy*, 1973. p. 46

Cohen, Leonard – Poet and songwriter Cohen is famous for his songs "Suzanne," "That's No Way to Say Goodbye," and "In My Life." An album, *The Best of Leonard Cohen*, was published in 1967, and in 1968 his *Selected Poems, 1956-1968*, appeared. p. 42

Contender, The – A 2000 movie starring Jeff Bridges as a US president seeking to fill a vice-presidential vacancy with a Republican-turned-Democrat senator, played by Joan Allen. The film asks powerful questions and makes a plea for integrity in public service. pp. 101, 128

Constitution of the Iroquois Confederacy – Among many versions of this document, one source is *The Constitution of the Five Nations – The Iroquois Book of the Great Law*, published by University of the State of New York, 1916, by Arthur C. Parker, archaeologist of the State Museum of New York. Historians debate the origin of The Great Law, some placing it between 1450 and 1500 CE, others placing it as early as 1390. pp. 12-14

D

Dahl, Susan – Wife of Jason Dahl, pilot, United Flight 93, 9/11/2001. p. 147

Davis, Wade – Ethno-botanist Davis traveled extensively in the Amazon and the Andes as a plant explorer and photographer. He co-authored *Earth Guide*, a 13-part television series aired on the Discovery Channel, and a recent documentary *Forests Forever*. p. 85

Declaration of Independence United States of America. p. 16

Declaration of Interdependence – Written by five members of the David Suzuki Foundation Team for the United Nations Earth Summit in Rio de Janeiro, 1994. p. 78

De Mille, Agnes – Legendary choreographer of ballet and dance for Broadway theatre productions, including: *Oklahoma*, *Carousel* and *Brigadoon*. In 1953, she founded the Agnes De Mille Theatre. p. 104

Deshpande, Nirmala – A peace activist and interfaith leader, Deshpande lives in India and is a leading scholar teaching the philosophy of Mahatma Gandhi. p. 154

Dewey, John – A leading American philosopher and educational theorist, Dewey is known for *School and Society* and *Democracy and Education*. In 1888, his essay "The Ethics of Democracy" appeared in the *University of Michigan Philosophical Papers*. pp. 22, 47, 129

Dionne, E.J. – Currently a columnist with the *Washington Post*. Dionne's expertise encompasses community, civil society, elections, faith- based initiatives and politics. Dionne wrote "United We Serve?," a debate over national service, *Brookings Review*, 2002. p. 131

Dobzhansky, Theodosius – A Russian-born geneticist and zoologist, Dobzhansky taught at the California Institute of Technology beginning in 1936. He posited that "it is possible there is, after all, something unique about man and the planet he inhabits." p. 94

Durant, Will – A macro-historian, Durant presents the reader with a broad conception of the issues he is covering. Among his works are *The Story of Philosophy*, 1983, and *The Age of Faith*, 2000. p. 93

E

Edelman, Marian Wright – Lawyer, educator and children's advocate, Edelman is founder and president of The Children's Defense Fund in Washington, DC. p. 157

Einstein Albert – Einstein's theory of the universe – his general theory of relativity – is credited with contributing to a revolution in science by overturning Newtonian views. His book *The General Theory of Relativity* was published in 1916, and he won the Nobel Prize for Physics in 1921. pp. 15, 158

Eisenhower, Dwight D. – The commanding general of the allied forces in World War II, Eisenhower served as 34th president of the US (1953-96). As president he was known for his moderate Republican policies and his enforcement of a court-ordered desegregation decision in Little Rock in 1957. p. 181

Eliot, George – One of the world's great novelists, Mary Ann Evans, wrote in 19th-century England using the name George Eliot, under which she published her brilliant novel *Middlemarch*, considered her masterpiece. p. 164

Emerson, Ralph Waldo – Leading 19th-century philosopher, poet and author, Emerson produced essays, proverbs, aphorisms, and maxims of abiding wisdom. Influenced by Transcendentalist thought, his essay "Nature," 1836, explores nature's mystical unity. pp. 85, 118, 138, 146

Englebart, Douglas – Computing pioneer Englebart is credited with inventing the computer mouse. He is founder of Bootstrap Institute, an organization that seeks to develop collaborative knowledge management practices. p. 167

F

Farrugia, Alastair – Maltese computer programmer with a doctorate in mathematics. p. 48

Fisher-Smith Jordan – A forest ranger living in California, Fisher-Smith has published several interviews with such famous environmental writers and activists as Jane Goodall, Wendell Berry and Al Gore. p. 80

Fleming, Maria – Editor of *A Place at the Table, Struggles for Equality in America*. p. 31

Fliss, Michael – Currently lives in Durham, North Carolina, and pursues Aikido, a martial art based on nonviolent principles. p. 176

Foe, Victoria Elizabeth – An independent university scholar and MacArthur Fellow, Foe studies fruit fly embryology. p. 83

Follett, Mary Parker – One of America's preeminent thinkers about democracy. Her ideas, generated in the early 20th century, remain fascinating today. Joan C. Tom produced Follett's recent biography: *Mary P. Follett, Creating Democracy and Transforming Management*, 2003. pp. 14-15, 69, 109, 115, 181

Fosdick, Harry Emerson – A liberal Protestant clergyman and persuasive preacher in the early 20th century, Fosdick was a pacifist, a champion of civil rights and the author of 47 books. p. 170

Fournier, Jim – Co-founder of PLANETWORK, a non-profit organization dedicated to applying information technology to pressing real work issues, focused on ecology, social justice and political self-determination. p. 172

Fox, Matthew – A spiritual theologian and visionary, Fox is founder of The University of Creation Spirituality in Oakland, California. Among his best-selling books are *Original Blessing* and *A Spirit Named Compassion*. p. 88

Frank, Billy – A fisherman and member of the Nisqually tribe, Frank works to find cooperative solutions to environmental problems and is chairman of the Northwest Indian Fisheries Commission. p. 161

Freire, Paolo – Brazilian educational philosopher Freire is one of the most influential 20th-century thinkers in education. His highly acclaimed book is *Pedagogy of the Oppressed*. p. 137

Fromm, Erich – 20th-century American psychoanalyst and social philosopher whose works include *Escape from Freedom*, *The Fear of Freedom* and *The Sane Society*. p. 90

G

Galbraith, John Kenneth – Modern economist Galbraith's provocative works include *The New Industrial State*, 1967; and *The Good Society*, 1996. p. 138

Gandhi, Mahatma – An attorney in India, Gandhi led India's struggle for independence from Britain and advocated a creed of passive resistance against injustice. Gandhi's philosophy of non-violence and living simply so that others may simply live remains a beacon for peace and justice movements worldwide. p. 120

Gleick, James – An author, reporter and essayist whose two books on science were Pulitzer Prize and National Book award finalists. Recent books include *Faster, The Acceleration of Just About Everything*. p. 92

Glendon, Mary Ann – Learned Hand Professor of Law at Harvard University, Glendon's publications include *A World Made New: Eleanor Roosevelt and the Universal Declaration of Human Rights*, 2001, and *Comparative Legal Traditions*, 1999. p. 185

Goethe, Johann Wolfgang von – A revered 18th-century dramatist. Among Goethe's best-known achievements is the play, *Faust.* Goethe lived in Weimar, Germany and directed the Weimar Theatre. p. 37

Goldberg, Whoopi – A wild and witty film and television actress and comedian, with a strong concern for social justice. p. 179

Gomez, Jason Thomas – Chairs California's Religious Diversity Forum in Orange County and is a leader in Be the Cause, a non-profit organization. He is pursuing a Masters in Theology to help usher in an age of religious reconciliation. p. 166

Graham, Martha – A monumental influence in 20th-century dance, Graham created the Martha Graham Dance Company, which trained and inspired generations of dancers. Her contributions transformed the world of dance. p. 114

Granoff, Jonathan, Esq. – President of the Global Security Institute. Granoff is author of *The Constitution, the Document that Created a Nation.* pp. 32, 150

Guevara, Ernesto Ché – A famous revolutionary, Guevara was a leader in the Cuban revolution. He left Cuba to set up a guerilla force in Bolivia and was killed there in 1967. p. 103

H

Haddock, Doris – Better known as Granny D, at age 90 Haddock completed a 3200-mile, 14-month walk across the United States to call attention to campaign finance reform. Her best-selling book is *Granny D, You're Never Too Old to Raise a Little Hell*, 2003. pp. 35, 133, 148, 175

Hale, Edward Everett – 19th-century author and Unitarian minister, Hale is famous for his short novel, *The Man Without a Country*, published in the *Atlantic Monthly* in 1863. p. 160

Hammarskjold, Dag – Elected United Nations Secretary General in 1953 and again in 1957, Hammarskjold was involved in conflicts on three continents and effectively used what he liked to call "preventive diplomacy." His personal journal, *Markings*, was published posthumously in 1963 and is described as "a collection of spiritual truths given in artistic form." p. 111

Hand, Learned – An honored US Federal Court Judge and strong advocate of free speech, he was often called "the 10th justice of the Supreme Court." Among his writings, Hand is recognized for *The Spirit of Liberty*, a series of his papers and addresses. p. 115

Havel, Vaclav – The first elected president of the Czech Republic (1993-2003), Havel has been awarded numerous international prizes for his literary work, civic activities and commitment to human rights. pp. 90, 130, 145

Hemingway, Ernest – A great 20th-century American writer. Among his works are the classic novels *The Sun Also Rises, A Farewell to Arms,* and his Pulitzer Prize-winning novella, *The Old Man and the Sea. p.* 36

Hightower, James – Author, radio commentator and public speaker, Hightower was twice elected to statewide office in Texas. He publishes a monthly political newsletter, *The Hightower Lowdown*. p. 76

Hindu Proverb. p. 164

H.H. the Dalai Lama – Recognized at the age of two as the reincarnation of the 13th Dalai Lama, he is universally acknowledged as one of the world's preeminent spiritual leaders and was awarded the Nobel Peace Prize in 1989. pp. 82, 85, 118

Hock, Dee – Founding CEO of VISA International, Hock is a laureate in the Business Hall of Fame for his innovations in organization and management. He is a writer, speaker and author of *Birth of the Chaordic Age*, 1999. pp. 63, 94, 177

Holmes, Jr., Oliver Wendell – Famed 19th-century American jurist, served as an associate justice of the US Supreme Court from 1902-1932. Because of his frequent differences with conservative members of the court over their efforts to nullify social legislation, he was nicknamed the Great Dissenter. pp. 48, 89

Horton, Miles – Established Highlander Folk School in East Tennessee in 1932 where he taught self-respect and self-empowerment to Appalachian miners and laborers. Later, Rosa Parks, Martin Luther King, Jr. and Andrew Young studied non-violent protest at Highlander. *The Long Haul, Autobiography of Miles Horton*, with Herbert and Judith Kohl, 1990, tells his story. p. 67

Housden, Roger – Author of *A Sacred America, The Emerging Spirit of the People* and *Sacred Journeys in the Modern World*. pp. 18, 116

Hubbard, Barbara Marx – Author and futurist. Hubbard's best-selling book is *Conscious Evolution, The Great Awakening, A Spirit Motivated Plan of Action for the 21st Century*. p. 106

Hughes, Langston – One of the 20th century's most significant black writers of poetry, prose and drama, Hughes consistently demonstrated inextinguishable hope to his fellow African Americans. p. 88

Hugo, Victor – French novelist, poet and playwright. Hugo's most famous works include *The Hunchback of Notre Dame* and *Les Miserables*. p. 92

Hume, David – 18th-century Scottish philosopher Hume wrote *Philosophical Essays Concerning Human Understanding*, 1748. p. 47

I

Inuit Song. p. 24

Ito Joichi – President and founder of Neoteny, Inc., an investment and operating company for Internet technology-related projects and ventures. p. 96

Ivins, Molly – Career journalist Ivins was a political reporter for the *New York Times* and currently works freelance. Her best-selling books, *Molly Ivins Can't Say That, Can She?* and *Nothin' But Good Lies Ahead*, both focus on politics and journalism. p. 106

J

Jackson, Robert – A one-time US Supreme Court justice, Jackson also served as Chief American Prosecutor at the Nuremberg trials following World War II and is acclaimed for setting new standards in international law. p. 50

Jacques, Zina – A former educator at Urban High School, San Francisco CA. p. 157

Janki, Dadi – A woman of wisdom, Dadi Janki is the Joint Administrative Head of the Brahma Kumaris World Spiritual University. Her writings include *Companion of God* and *Wings of Soul: Releasing our Spiritual Identity* and *The World and Wisdom of Dadi Janki*,1999. p. 69

Jeffers, Susan – Best-selling author of self-help books including *Feel the Fear and Do It Anyway*. p. 36

Jefferson, Thomas – Third president of the US (1801-1809), Jefferson drafted the Declaration of Independence and contributed to the Constitutional Convention. A powerful advocate of liberty, Jefferson said, "I have sworn upon the altar of God eternal hostility against every form of tyranny over the mind of man." pp. 23, 132

Jesus of Nazareth, John 13:34 RSV. p. 153

Johnson, Sarah – 10th-grade student as quoted by Roger Housden in *Sacred America, The Emerging Spirit of the People. p.* 117

Johnson, Steven – Editor-in-chief of *Feed*, an award-winning online cultural magazine. p. 97

Joyer, Sharon and Pat Nagle – A Catholic sister, Joyer is a teacher and co-founder with Pat Nagle of the Lilly Luckett neighborhood garden in Oakland, CA. Pat Nagle, also a Catholic sister, is a community organizer. p. 84

Jung, Carl – A renowned early 20th-century psychoanalyst, Jung was a student of Sigmund Freud. He pioneered work that made sense of the unconscious and its habit of revealing itself through symbols. Most of his writings are found in *The Collected Works of Carl Jung.* p. 76

K

Kabir – A great mystic poet of India in the 15th century. Kabir's philosophy represents a synthesis of Hindu and Muslim concepts. One source for his work is *The Kabir Book, Forty-Four of the Ecstatic Poems of Kabir*, edited by Robert Bly. p. 121

Keillor, Garrison – One of America's favorite storytellers, Keillor hosts the popular radio program *A Prairie Home Companion* and has published several books. p. 109

Keller, Helen – Unable from the time she was two to hear or see, Keller became a world leader, an international hero, and a staunch advocate for civil rights, human dignity and world peace. pp. 35, 163

Kemmis, Daniel – Former Montana legislator and mayor of Missoula, Kemmis directs the Center for Rocky Mountain West at the University of Montana. His recent books are *Community and the Politics of Place* and *The Good City and the Good Life.* p. 53

Kennedy, John Fitzgerald – 35th President of the US (1961-1963), Kennedy inspired his generation of Americans to offer their best service in the cause of human rights. Kennedy was assassinated November 22, 1963. His book *Profiles in Courage*, 1955, won the Pulitzer Prize in History. pp. 71, 158, 184

Kennedy, Robert F. – Attorney General of the United States (1961-1964), Kennedy was an untiring advocate for human rights at home and abroad. He was slain June 5, 1968, at age 42, shortly after claiming victory in California's Democratic primary. pp. 30, 39, 144-145, 163, 182

King, Jr., Martin Luther – Clergyman, civil rights leader, intellectual and social reformer, King pointed out the flaws in America and offered a roadmap for justice. King advanced the cause of civil rights and spoke against the Vietnam War. He won the Nobel Prize for Peace in 1964. pp. 54, 60, 76, 91, 121, 132, 142, 156

Kirpalini, Jayanti and Panjabi Mohini – Teachers with the Brahma Kumaris World Spiritual University, a movement located in Mt. Abu, India, and in centers all over the world. p. 157

Koestler, Arthur – A 20th-century world citizen, novelist, political activist and social philosopher. Two of his most compelling books are the novel *Darkness at Noon*, 1941, and his journal, *The Lotus and the Robot*, 1960. p. 100

Kuralt, Charles – A popular and gifted travel and news correspondent, Kuralt traveled American highways and brought fresh and engaging glimpses of everyday life into people's living rooms. p. 147

L

Lappé, Francis Moore – Food activist and author, Lappé founded the Center for a Living Democracy in Vermont. Best known for her book *Diet for a Small Planet*. Lappé's recent book is *Hope's Edge, The Next Diet for a Small Planet*. pp. 38-39, 52-53, 133

Lazarus, Emma – American Jewish poet whose poem "The New Colossus," 1883, is engraved on the plaque at the base of the Statue of Liberty and has inspired generations of Americans and immigrants to the US. p. 65

Lee, Harper – Lee's quotation comes from her best-selling novel, *To Kill a Mockingbird*, published in 1960, and soon made into a major film. Lee was awarded an honorary doctorate by Spring Hill College in her home state of Alabama in 1997, for "lyrical elegance and her portrayal of human strength and wisdom." p. 34

Lincoln, Abraham – Revered in history for his extraordinary leadership during the US Civil War, which restored the Union and ended slavery in the South, Lincoln served as the 16th president of the US from 1861 until his assassination in 1865. pp. 34, 119, 174

Littlesun, Roy – a speaker and teacher from the Hopi Tradition, Littlesun made a 108 day world tour for east-west union and world peace in 1996. p. 77

Loeb, Paul – Esteemed writer on social involvement, Loeb's recent books are, *Soul of A Citizen, Living with Conviction in a Cynical Time* and *The Impossible Will Take a Little While.* p. 37

Lozoff, Bo – With his wife, Sita, Lozoff founded the Human Kindness Foundation in 1987, which stresses a way of life based upon simple living, dedication to service, and a commitment to personal spiritual practice. His recent books are *We're All Doing Time* and *It's a Meaningful Life, It Just Takes Practice.* p. 150

Luxen, Andrew – Contributor to 2020 Vision, Luxen graduated from the University of Colorado in 2001, worked for US Representative Rosa de Lauro and plans to attend University of Denver Law School. *www.2020Democrats.org*, p. 50

Lyons, Oren – A traditional faith keeper of the Turtle Clan and a member of the Onondaga, Lyons is a professor of American Studies at the State University of New York, Buffalo, where he directs the Native American Studies Program. p. 131

M

Maathai, Wangari – A respected activist who fought fearlessly for the environment and social justice in Africa. Maathai is the founder of The Green Belt Movement in Kenya and is a leader of the National Council of Women in Kenya. p. 102

Machado, Antonio – 20th-century Spanish poet Machado's published works include *Time Alone: Selected Poems* and *Border of a Dream, Selected Poems of Antonio Machado*. p. 124

MacLeish, Archibald – Major American poet and dramatist MacLeish also held several political posts under President Franklin Roosevelt, including librarian of Congress, and won a Pulitzer Prize in 1952 for his *Collected Poems, 1917-1952*. p. 170

Macy, Joanna – An eco-philosopher and a scholar of Buddhism and systems theory. Her books include *Coming Back to Life: Practices to Reconnect Our Lives; Our World and World as Lover, World as Self;* and *Mutual Causality in Buddhism and Systems Theory*. pp. 40, 77

Madison, James – Delegate to the Constitutional Convention, contributor to the Federalist papers, and fourth president of the US (1809-1817). When Madison was called "the father of the Constitution," he protested: "This document," he said, "was not the off-spring of a single brain but the work of many heads and many hands." pp. 16, 17

Mandela, Nelson – Accepted the Nobel Peace Prize in 1993 on behalf of all of the South Africans who suffered and sacrificed to bring peace to their land. After years of imprisonment for his leadership against apartheid, Mandela became the president of South Africa (1994-1999). His 1994 autobiography is *Long Walk to Freedom*. p. 45

Manville, Brook and Josiah Ober – History scholars and co-authors of *A Company of Citizens, What the World's First Democracy Teaches Leaders about Creating Great Organizations*. The authors call for a greater democracy in the workplace. p. 22

Marsalis, Wynton – Named by *Time* magazine in 1996 as one of America's most influential people, Marsalis was the first jazz musician to win the Pulitzer Prize. He also has won eight Grammy awards for his jazz and classical recordings; is artistic director for Jazz at New York's Lincoln Center; and makes musical education for young audiences a top priority. p. 102

Marshall, Thurgood – Won the most important legal case of the 20th century, Brown v. Board of Education, which ended the legal separation of black and white children in public schools. Marshall was appointed to the US Supreme Court in 1967 and served the court until 1991. p. 63

Mattison, Avon – International PeaceBuilder Mattison is founder and president of Pathways to Peace, a non-profit organization in consultative status with the United Nations. p. 162

May, Rollo – The writings of noted existentialist psychologist May include *The Meaning of Anxiety*, 1950, *Psychology and the Human Dilemma*, 1967, and *Love and Will*, 1969. p. 130

McCrary, P.K. – A professional storyteller living in Houston, Texas, McCrary promotes stories of peace and justice. p. 107

McKibbon, Bill – An author and an environmental activist. His book *The End of Nature, Tenth Anniversary Edition* was first published in 1989. p. 82

Mead, Margaret – Noted anthropologist, explorer and writer, Mead is known for *Coming of Age in Samoa*, 1928, and *Culture and Commitment*, 1978. Mead said, "I have spent most of my life studying the lives of other peoples – faraway peoples – so that Americans might better understand themselves." pp. 59, 60

Meadows, Donella – A systems analyst, journalist and Ph.D. in biophysics, Meadows is known for a nationally syndicated newspaper column, *The Global Citizen*. p. 83

Merton, Thomas – The classic works of this Trappist monk, poet, social activist and prolific writer are his autobiography, *The Seven Storey Mountain*, and *Seeds of Contemplation*. Contact *www.merton.org* p. 61

Mindell, Arnold – Author and shaman Mindell discusses shamanism in many aspects of western life such as therapy, medicine and partnering. His works include *Dreaming While Awake*, *Quantum Mind*, and *Riding the Horse Backwards, Process Work in Theory and Practice*. p. 81

Mohamed – A teenaged boy currently living in Palestine. pp. 166-167

Mohini, Panjabi. See Kirpalini, Jayanti and Panjabi Mohini.

Moyers, Bill – Television journalist Moyers established Public Affairs Television in 1986 and has produced award-winning documentaries, including *In Search of the Constitution; Listening to America with Bill Moyers, Creativity*, and *A Walk Through the 20th Century*. pp. 20, 38, 110, 180

Muir, John – Conservationist and founder of The Sierra Club, Muir described himself as a "poetico-trampo-geologist-botanist and ornithologist-naturalist, etc!" p. 75

Muller, Robert – Former Undersecretary General of the United Nations. His recent books are *New Genesis, Shaping a Global Spirituality*, and *What the War Taught Me about Peace;* and, his biography, *Prophet, The Hatmaker's Son*. Websites: *www.robertmuller.org* and *www.goodmorningworld.org*. p. 44

Mumford, Lewis – A 20th-century writer and lecturer on social problems, Mumford furthered the ideal of local involvement with global vision. His autobiography is *My Work and My Days: A Personal Chronicle*, 1979. p. 93

Muslim Hadith [Sacred teaching]. p. 130

N

Nachmanovitch, Stephen – Author, musician, and computer artist, Nachmanovitch wrote *Free Play, Improvisation in Life and Art*, 1990, and more recently published computer software, The World Music Menu and Music Tone Painter. pp. 100, 108

Nagle, Pat. See Joyer, Sharon and Pat Nagle.

Needleman, Jacob – Best-selling author of *The American Soul, Money and the Meaning of Life, Lost Christianity*, and *A Little Book on Love*, Needleman is a professor of philosophy at San Francisco State University. pp. 17, 20, 137

New Testament Apocrypha. p. 125

Nelson, Linda – Renovator of an opera house in a small town in Maine. p. 52

Neruda, Pablo – 1971 recipient of the Nobel Prize for Literature, this great Chilean poet's extensive works include 250 poems organized in fifteen literary cycles and translated into ten languages. p. 81

Niebuhr, Reinhold – A social ethics professor at Union Theological Seminary for four decades, Niebuhr's most famous books include *Moral Man in Immoral Society*, 1932, *Christianity and Power Politics*, 1940, and *The Nature and Destiny of Man* (2 vol., 1941-1943). p. 148

Norton, Eleanor Holmes – African-American lawyer and United States Congresswoman representing the District of Columbia. Before her election to Congress in 1990, Norton broke several gender and racial barriers in her legal career, as she defended the rights of others for equal opportunity and freedom of speech. p. 88

O

Ober, Josiah. See Manville, Brook and Josiah Ober.

Oliver, Mary – A contemporary American poet known for her attentiveness to the simple and astonishing occurrences in nature. Oliver won the Pulitzer Prize with *American Primitive* in 1984, and her *New and Selected Poems* won the National Book Award in 1992. p. 106

Olsen, Milton – A naturalist whose instructive, popular essay "Lessons from Geese" deals with human behavior. p. 81

P

Paine, Thomas – A British/American writer and a major figure in the American Revolutionary War. Paine is known for his works *Common Sense* and *The Rights of Man*. pp. 15, 17, 65, 103, 131

Paz, Octavio – Mexican poet and diplomat, Paz received the Nobel Prize for Literature in 1990. His poem "Sun Shone (Piedra de Sol)" is one of the most remarkable in his ten volumes of work. p. 96

Peoples, Tricia – A community organizer and former leader of the Louisiana Bucket Brigade, a citizens' action group that successfully forced Shell Oil to give fair treatment to families living next to a refinery in Norco, Louisiana. p. 136

Pericles – Athenian statesman, general, and orator. Under his leadership, in the 5th century BCE, Athens' prosperity, democratic reforms, and physical beauty brought the era such renown that it was known as the Golden Age of Athens. p. 21

Perlman, Itzhak – World-renowned violinist Perlman is the winner of four Emmy Awards and beloved for his impeccable technique and his irrepressible joy in making music. A recent release is *Classical Perlman, Rhapsody*. p. 107

Peters, Ralph – A retired U.S. Army officer and expert on the "covert, the classified, and the catastrophic" is author of *Beyond Terror, Strategy in a Changing World*. p. 123

Pir Vilayat Inayat Khan – The eldest son and successor to the founder of the Sufi Order in the West, Pir Valayat's teachings bring the timeless contributions of the ancient Sufi mystics and poets together with the discoveries of psychology and science. Among his books is *Awakening*, 1999. p. 122

Plato – Considered one of the greatest philosophers of all time, Plato was an associate of Socrates and founded the Academy, over which he presided for 40 years, and where both men and women were his students. Plato's major works include *The Republic* and *The Dialogues*. p. 21

Populist Party – Also called The People's Party, was established in 1892, when delegates from farm and labor groups met to protest falling farm prices. They advocated public ownership of railroads, steamships, telephone and telegraph and free coinage of silver, but after some of their demands were met and farm prices began to rise, the party dissolved. p. 64

Populist Platform, The. p. 162 (also, see Populist Party, above)

Porto, André – A spiritual activist and interfaith community organizer, Porto works for Viva Rio, the largest non-profit social service organization in Rio de Janeiro. pp. 55, 177-178

Proverbs 6:6-8. p. 98

R

Rainer, Howard – A Native American originally from Taos Pueblo, New Mexico. His book *Whisperings of the Heart, Prose to Uplift the Human Spirit* explains Rainer's desire "that the simplicity of his word will lift someone's spirit in trying times." pp. 41, 168

Ram Dass – The recent books of spiritual teacher and modern sage Ram Dass include *Be Here Now;* and *Still Here, Embracing Change, Aging and Dying.* p. 145

Ratcliffe, Mitch –Writer and entrepreneur based in the Pacific Northwest; leading commentator on the economy and technology. p. 98

Regional Plan Association, Region at Risk – First unveiled in 1996, this plan was an urgent call to public and private sector leaders in three states, New York, New Jersey, and Connecticut, to work together to reverse deteriorating economic and environmental condition in the tri-state area. p. 79

Reinsborough, Patrick – Author of *Beyond Voting, Building a Real Democracy in an Age of Empire* and co-founder of Smart Meme Strategy and Training Project. p. 109

Remen, Rachel Naomi – A clinical professor of family and community medicine at the University of California, San Francisco, Remen co-founded the Commonweal Cancer Help Program. Her best-selling books are *Kitchen Table Wisdom, Stories that Heal,* 2000, and *My Grandfather's Blessing,* 2001. p. 124

Reyna, Tony – Twice governor of Taos Pueblo, survivor of the World War II Bataan Death March, civic leader. p. 165

Rilke, Rainer Maria – The greatest lyric poet of 20th-century Germany, Rilke first achieved fame with his *Poems from the Book of Hours*, 1905; and his renowned *Duino Elegies*, 1923, embodies his highest praise of human existence. p. 152

Ritchlin, Sheri – Ph.D, dream analyst, scholar in Asian philosophy, and spiritual teacher, Ritchlin provides in her book *One-ing*, 2004, an elegant crystallization of wisdom from the I Ching. pp. 129, 134, 152, 153

Roosevelt, Eleanor – Remarkable first lady and wife of President Franklin Delano Roosevelt, her historic accomplishment was to help write The Universal Declaration of Human Rights, completed in 1948. Her writings are found in *Courage to Live in A Dangerous World, The Political Writings of Eleanor Roosevelt*, edited by Allida M. Black. pp. 32, 41, 42, 64, 122-123, 139, 143

Roosevelt, Franklin Delano – 32nd president of the US, Roosevelt served from 1933-1945. He brought relief to Americans during the Depression through economic reforms, advanced New Deal legislation, and led the nation through World War II. He devoted much of his attention to developing the United Nations and working towards world peace. pp. 70, 136

Rogers, Will – Beloved 20th-century American humorist. In addition to his work in movies, on the radio, and as a newspaper columnist, Rogers wrote books that include *The Cowboy Philosopher on Prohibition*, 1919, and *The Illiterate Digest*, 1924. pp. 94, 160

Rogue Valley Wisdom Council – First met in 2003 in Medford, Oregon and is dedicated to bringing new life to democracy. pp. 66-67

Royster, Whitney – Newspaper correspondent in the Rocky Mountain west. pp. 172-173.

Rumi, Mevlana Jalaluddin—13th-century mystic, spiritual master, poet and founder of the Mawlawi Sufi order, whose sumptuous poetry is still read worldwide today. When he died on December 17, 1273, men of five faiths followed his bier. pp. 111, 121

Russell, Bertrand – English philosopher Russell's works include *An Inquiry into the Meaning and Truth* and *A History of Western Philosophy*. He did influential work in mathematical logic and received the Nobel Prize for Literature in 1952. p. 95

S

Sagarmatha Declaration, Nepal – Adopted at the International Consultation on Water Resource Development in South Asia and included in the Report of the World Commission on Dams, December 8-10, 2002, Kathmandu, Nepal. p. 70

Said, Abdul Aziz – As the senior ranking professor at American University in Washington, DC, Said founded and directs the International Peace and Conflict Resolution Program and the university-wide Center for Global Peace. p. 25

St. Francis of Assisi – Son of a wealthy family, St. Francis converted to Catholicism at age 22 and took up a clearly ascetic life. He later founded the Franciscan Order in the 13th century, and exemplified simplicity of life, love of poverty, religious fervor, and humility before God p. 144

St. Ignatius Loyola – Founded the Society of Jesus (Jesuits), a Catholic order of priests, in the 16th century. Loyola produced *Spiritual Exercises*, which recognize that not only intellect but also emotions and feelings help us come to know actions of spirit in our lives. p. 119

Sanchez, Stephanie, Dave Leahy, Yael Muhlrad, young Democratic visionaries. p. 183

Sandburg, Carl – American writer and poet Sandburg received the Pulitzer Prize in 1940 for his biography *Abraham Lincoln, The Prairie Years* and *Abraham Lincoln, The War Years;* and again in 1951, for *Complete Poems*. Among his other works are *The People, Yes!* and *Chicago Poems*. pp. 142, 179

Sawin, Beth – Mother, biologist and systems analyst, Sawin works at the Sustainability Institute in Hartland, Vermont. To receive her monthly column in systems and sustainability, contact *bethsawin@vermontel.net*. p. 51

Schweickart, Rusty – NASA astronaut who served as lunar module pilot on Apollo 9, Schweickart was founder and past president of The Association of Space Explorers, a group that promotes the cooperative exploration of space and use of space technology for human benefit. The Association's book *Home Planet*, 1988, was a bestseller. p. 62

Schweitzer, Albert – Awarded the Nobel Peace Prize in 1952, Schweitzer used his prize money to expand his hospital in French Equatorial Africa and to build a leper colony. He wrote, "man must cease attributing his problems to his environment and learn to exercise his will – his personal responsibility." p. 77

Seneca – Roman Stoic philosopher and statesman who died in 65 CE. Although he was a Stoic, he was inclined more toward wise and practical conduct than toward abstract speculation. p. 170

Shaw, George Bernard – Irish dramatist Shaw was a leading figure in 20th-century theatre and was awarded the Nobel Prize for Literature in 1925. Among his most famous works are *Pygmalion*, *Saint Joan*, *Major Barbara*, and *Arms and the Man*. p. 123

Sitting Bull – Lakota chief and holy man, Sitting Bull was widely respected for his bravery and insight. Sitting Bull received a vision that foretold an Indian victory at the Battle of Little Big Horn in 1876. p. 58

Socrates – A 5th-century BCE philosopher living in Athens, Socrates did not leave writings, but his teachings were transmitted in the works of Plato. In Plato's dialogue *The Phaedo*, Socrates holds that life must be lived with a view to the "cultivation of the soul." p. 63

Springsteen, Bruce – Legendary rock and roll guitarist and singer-songwriter. "The Boss" has sold millions of albums worldwide including *Born to Run* in 1974 and *Born in the USA* a decade later. p. 178

Steffens, Lincoln – US journalist at the turn of the 20th century, referred to as a "muckracker" for his exposition of local government corruption. Steffens' books include an autobiography, *The Shame of the Cities*, 1904, and *The Struggle for Self-Government*, 1906. p. 184

Stevenson, Adlai E. – Twice a Democratic candidate for President, Stevenson was regarded as one of the greatest orators of his time. He earlier served as Governor of Illinois, and, in 1961, was appointed by John F. Kennedy to be Ambassador to the United Nations, in which post he served until his death in 1965. p. 26

Storm, Hymeyohst, – The books of contemporary Native American writer Storm include *Seven Arrows*, *Song of Heyoehkah*, and *Lightningbolt*. p. 124

Strickland, William – President and CEO of the Manchester Bidwell Corporation, Strickland founded the Bidwell Training Center and Manchester Craftsmen's Guild, which trains and educates chronically unemployed and disadvantaged people in Pittsburgh, PA. p. 117

Swedish Proverb. p. 165

Swimme, Brian – Mathematician and cosmologist, Swimm teaches at the California Institute of Integral Studies, San Francisco. Among his published works are *The Hidden Heart of the Cosmos* (also a video series) and *The Universe Story* with collaborator and cultural historian Thomas Berry. His media work also includes the video series *Canticle to the Cosmos*. p. 27

Sylvus, William H. – Founder of the Iron Moulders' Union, one of the earliest labor unions in the US. p. 156

T

Tagore, Rabindranath – The first Indian to receive the Nobel Prize for Literature, in 1913, Tagore was one of modern India's greatest poets and the composer of the Indian national anthem. p. 44

Taylor, Alan John Percival – Popular English historian Taylor is known for his lecture presentations on television. His final lecture was *How Wars End*, 1985. p. 49

Taylor, Glenda – A biochemist and professor at Tulane University. p. 79

Teilhard de Chardin, Pierre – A 20th-century Jesuit priest and distinguished pale-ontologist, Teilhard de Chardin integrated scientific research with religious vocation. His best-known works are *The Phenomenon of Man, Christianity and Evolution;* and *The Divine Milieu, An Essay on the Interior Life.* pp. 24, 125, 146, 154

The Talmud. p. 48

Thich Nhat Hanh – A Vietnamese Buddhist monk, Thich Nhat Hanh received the Nobel Peace Prize in 1964 and was nominated again for the prize in 1967. His writings include *Peace is Every Step: The Path of Mindfulness in Everyday Life* and *Living Buddha, Living Christ.* pp. 114, 122

Thurber, James – Gifted cartoonist and humorist, Thurber wrote the "casuals" for the *New Yorker* magazine – short pieces about his own experiences. Stories of Thurber's day-to-day life in Columbus, Ohio, somewhat embellished, are found in his *My Life and Hard Times,* 1973. p. 74

Tocqueville, Alexis de – Student of democracy Tocqueville left France at age 25 and traveled in the US for nine months in 1831. From his travels he wrote *Democracy in America,* a landmark masterpiece of political observation and analy-sis of democracy in the US. pp. 30, 161

Truitt, Anne – A contemporary artist, Truitt challenges the conventions of tra-ditional painting and sculpture. Her published journals include *Daybook, Turn,* and *Prospect.* p. 54

Tutu, Desmond – South African Anglican bishop and fierce critic of apartheid, Tutu spoke out for peaceful negotiated reconciliation between black and white communities. He was awarded the Nobel Prize for Peace in 1984. pp. 74-75, 182

U

Underhill, Evelyn – A teacher and writer in England, Underhill applied her life to spiritual thought and practice. Her first important book was *Mysticism,* 1911. p. 168

United States Constitution, Preamble. p. 19

Upits, Andrejs – A 20th-century Latvian writer, Upits, who died in 1970, wrote about.the struggle between old and new Latvian generations. A major work of his is *Green Land*. p. 134

V

Van Gelder, Sara Ruth – Executive editor of *Yes! A Journal of Positive Futures*. p. 53

Vanier, Jean – Founder of L'Arche communities, faith-based homes for the poor and rejected people of society. Beginning with one home in 1964, there are now more than120 L'Arche communities in 30 countries. p. 89

Vargas, Roberto – Psychologist, facilitator and Chicano ceremonial leader, Vargas writes, "While my purpose has been to advance justice for my own community, I now see that it is time to also claim my stake in our nation's evolution. It's time for me to reclaim America." He is principal consultant for New World Associates and founder of the Porvida Council, which works to integrate the practice of spirit connection and cultural activism. p. 68

Von Hugel, Friedrich – A Roman Catholic religious writer and spiritual director whose writings include *The Mystical Element of Religion as Studied in St. Catherine of Genoa and Her Friends*, 1908. pp. 78, 150

W

Wagner, Ramon – Milwaukee community organizer. p. 149

Walljasper, Jay – Editor at-large of *The Utne Reader*, an alternative, independent magazine. p. 40

Walsh, Roger – A professor of psychiatry and human behavior at the University of California, Irvine. Walsh's research includes Asian psychology and philosophy, effects of meditation, and the psychology of religion. His books include *Paths Beyond Ego: The Transpersonal Vision*, 1993. p. 119

Wheatley, Margaret – Writes, teaches and speaks about radically new practices and ideas for organizing in chaotic times. She is president of The Berkana Institute and author of *Leadership and the New Science*; and *A Simpler Way*, co-authored with Myron Kellner-Rogers. pp. 61, 97, 104, 151

White, John – Author of *Meeting of Spirit and Science, Guidelines for a New Age*, White is general editor of Paragon House Omega Series. p. 23

Whitehead, Alfred North—co-author with Bertrand Russell of the three volumes of *Principia Mathematica*. His main interest was in the "no-man's land" between mathematics and philosophy. p. 105

Whitman, Walt – One of America's greatest poets, Whitman sang the praises of democracy, the dignity of the individual and the brotherhood of humanity. His work *Leaves of Grass* is considered one of the most influential volumes of poetry in the history of American literature. p. 67

Wilber, Ken – A comprehensive philosophical thinker, Ken Wilber has written over 16 books, including *A Brief History of Everything*, 1996, and *The Collected Works of Ken Wilber*, Vols 1-8, 2000. p. 135

Williams, Tennessee – Acclaimed Southern writer, author of *The Glass Menagerie*, 1945, and *A Streetcar Named Desire*, 1947. One of America's greatest playwrights, Williams also wrote two novels, short stories, and verse. p. 183

Williamson, Marianne – Best-selling author of *Healing the Soul of America, A Return to Love*, and *Everyday Grace*, Williamson directs Global Renaissance Alliance, dedicated to the belief that "every generation of Americans must rediscover for themselves the values, privileges, and responsibilities of American democracy." pp. 18, 45, 54, 116

Wills, Garry – Prolific writer of American history, Wills won the Pulitzer Prize for his book *Lincoln at Gettysburg*. His other books include *Certain Trumpets* and *James Madison: The American President Series*. p. 175

Wilson, Woodrow – 28th president of the US (1913-1921), Wilson led reform legislation that prohibited child labor and limited railroad workers to an eight hour day. He announced US entrance into World War I, a war "to make the world safe for democracy." pp. 115, 128, 137

Wordsworth, William – Considered one of the world's greatest poets, Wordsworth helped define the English Romantic movement in the early 19th century. p. 143

Y

Yogananda, Paramahansa – Author of the 1946 classic *Autobiography of a Yogi*, Yogananda was born in India, trained in yoga and sent to the West by his teachers. In 1925, he established the Self-Realization Fellowship near Los Angeles to facilitate the dissemination of his teachings. p. 91

Young, Margaret – Author of *House without Walls* (1991), *Salvador* (1992), and *Elegies and Love Songs* (1992). She teaches writing at Brigham Young University. p. 135

Z

Zumberg, Jerrin – Contributor to 2020 Vision, Zumberg says of himself, "as soon as you label me one thing I am every contradiction of that, so unfortunately no stereotype really fits my description." *www.2020Democrats.org*. p. 66

Are you inspired to become an active agent of change?

Here are a few suggestions to get started:

- Register to vote
- Volunteer on local civic projects
- Write a thank you note to your favorite champion of democracy
- Make a contribution to a civic group or politician whom you admire
- Participate in small group discussion. Ask each other questions like this:

  What was your earliest memory of democracy?

  What in your life experience stands out as a time when you were involved in something that made a difference?

  What leader of democracy (past or present) would you invite to a dinner party? Why?

  Imagine it is twenty years from today and a greater democracy has been born in your land. What is happening? What has changed?

- Post your ideas, connect with other readers, browse website links on our website www.democracyblog.org.

May this little book encourage you to fulfill your aspirations, enjoy your life and help make a better world.

Sally and Kathy